Thanks for being part of my day
March 26, 2018

7 BIG SECRETS

An Insider's Guide to:

Closing

Using the Phone

Getting Referrals

Overcoming Objections

Seminars

Leads

10 Prospecting Programs

Prospecting Concepts

BILL HARRIS

President, W.V.H., Inc.

Published by W.V.H., Inc.
San Diego, California

7 BIG SECRETS An Insider's Guide to: *Closing, Using the Phone, Getting Referrals, Overcoming Objections, Seminars, Leads, 10 Prospecting Programs, Prospecting Concepts*

Published by W.V.H., Inc.
10626 Falcon Rim Point, San Diego, California, 92131

2018 Edition - Eighth Printing

Book Editing: Rosemary Horvath

Cover Image: istockphoto.com/AK2

ISBN: 978-0-9844487-2-2
Library of Congress Control Number: 2010924409

About the Author

Bill Harris is President of W.V.H., Inc.

Bill Harris is the founder of 5 different companies; companies that wrote over 1 billion dollars of annuity premium. Bill has appeared in *Money Magazine* and in *The Wall Street Journal*, on TV and radio, in State Superior Court as an annuity expert witness, and "on stage" as one of the most sought after speakers with over 3,000 seminars and web conferences under his belt. Bill is the founder and president of W.V.H., Inc., a consulting and intellectual services company that licenses sales concepts, training tools, and creative media to some of the largest companies in the financial services industry. W.V.H., Inc., has created over 100 CD-ROMs and DVD-ROMs, has published ten books, and has produced many informative short films about the economy, inflation, Social Security, and saving.

See the last 2 pages for W.V.H., Inc.'s Books, Audio CD Library, and DVD-ROM

Important Message

You will soon learn many of the same approaches, words, techniques that 2,000 insurance and investment professionals used to write over 10 billion dollars of annuity, life and health insurance premium. As a result, you will now have almost everything you need to master the art of selling in one easy-to-read book.

The book is conveniently divided into 5 sections:

1. The first 6 BIG Secrets cover every aspect to selling. (Please see opposite page for more details)

2. Secret 7 could be a book by itself since it unveils 10 unique, proven or forgotten Prospecting Programs. (Please see opposite page)

3. The bonus section contains 7 more secrets (Please see opposite page)

4. Pages 261-294 are priceless since we tell you the 5 best people to call everyday and what to say to them. Because of these 30 pages, you will never again say that you have no one to call.

5. We end the book with some of our best Prospecting Concepts; concepts that can make prospecting so so easy.

This book helps two types of producers. The novice will learn in 30 days what took others a career to learn. And, seasoned producers get a library of the best of the best words, phrases, approaches, and forgotten strategies in one book.

At the least, this book will enhance your career. At the most, it will change your life.

Quick Summary

In this book you will learn:

Secret 1 You can learn how to close like the most successful producers do.

Secret 2 You can use the phone like a pro to prospect, make appointments, and sell.

Secret 3 You can get referrals consistently.

Secret 4 You can overcome almost any objection at the point of sale.

Secret 5 You can have a lot of success with public speaking.

Secret 6 You can have success with Leads.

Secret 7 You can triple your income by using some of these Prospecting Programs.

    1. Online Birthday Marketing
    2. Consumer Webinars
    3. The Most Overlooked Generation
    4. Client Appreciation Events
    5. The Names of the Most Overlooked People Are In Your File Cabinet
    6. Hallmark Birthday Cards
    7. Email Campaigns
    8. Direct Mail
    9. Radio Show Interview
   10. Television

BONUS!

Secret 8 You can have even more phone success by using these phone scripts.

Secret 9 You can now overcome any objection about surrender charges if you use this material.

Secret 10 You can get up to 80% of the seminar audience to want to get together with you.

Secret 11 You can use this formula for success.

Secret 12 You can find new annuity dollars by using the right approach.

Secret 13 You can learn a lot from history.

Secret 14 You can have more success if you have these words on your business card.

The Next 30 Days: A day-to-day calendar that tells you the 5 best people to call that day.

Prospecting Concepts Discover in minutes what took us 4 decades to learn, refine, and almost master.

Thank You

To Rosemary Horvath for working non-stop during the important "crunch days".

To Susan Humason for caring and wanting the best for us.

To Jackson Harris and Ella Rose (my grandchildren ages 8 and 5 respectively) for doing some online research and for just asking if they can help. To our newest grandchildren, Holden and Delphine, both born in 2017 for giving me the inspiration to enhance this book and to write our first children's book, "Luna's New Neighbors."

And, to my entire family, Mary, my wife, my children, Elizabeth, Will, and Chris, and to my son-in-law, Gregory, for his cooperation and to my new daughter-in-law, Evaleen, for her input on how our Secret books should look.

Again, thanks to all of you!

Table of Contents

Table of Contents

(continued)

Table of Contents
(continued)

Please see the last 2 pages for more W.V.H., Inc. Books, Audio CDs, and DVD-ROM.

secret **1**

You can learn how to close like the most successful producers do.

I n order to become really successful, we must know how to close. We must learn who to ask, when to ask, and how to ask. Please mentally replay the last unsuccessful sales interview you had. Did you ask the right way? With Secret #1, you'll learn 5 things you must do before any close will work, the importance of using "test closes" in your presentation, and you'll learn the closes that some of America's most successful annuity, life and health producers used to write billions of annuity, life and health premium. In short, you'll learn closing strategies that can enhance your career: Maybe, change your life.

1

You can learn how to close like the most successful producers do.

The definition of a great closer

Closing is one area in the selling profession which is continually misunderstood. Is a great closer manipulative? No! Is a great closer too aggressive? No!

A great closer is one who knows how to move customers toward decisions which are in the best interests of the customer.

Allow me to ask 3 questions. What was the largest annuity or life insurance case that you ever wrote? Were you happy the day you wrote that case? And, have you spent the commissions you earned on that case?

Now let's look at your client. They bought an annuity that has increased, increased, and increased and how much in income taxes have they paid on the tax-deferred accumulation? Not a penny! So who is real winner? Not you, you spent the commissions. The real winner is the consumer who is enjoying the benefits of owning the product that you recommended.

A great closer knows how to move a prospect toward making a wise decision.

One of the obstacles we face: Acting

Acting involves a change. Change involves a new insurance company, new premium and a new insurance and investment professional. People do not like change and the best way not to change is to say, "I want to think about it," or "Let me read the brochure first." These are great one-liners that prospects say because they can remain non-confrontational. They get what they think they want, no change. Therefore, one of the keys to closing is learning how to help prospects see that change is good. Change can help people get what they want such as less income taxes now, more money later, lifetime income, protecting the people they love, mortgage protection, college for their children, business continuation etc.

On the following page, we have a homework assignment for you. Please list as many benefits as you can to owning annuities, life insurance, and health insurance.

Homework Assignment
Please list the benefits to owning Annuities, Life Insurance, and Health Insurance

Annuity

1. *Less current taxes*
2. *More money later*
3. _____
4. _____
5. _____

6. _____
7. _____
8. _____
8. _____
10. _____

Life

1. *Protect the people you love*
2. *Mortgage protection*
3. _____
4. _____
5. _____

6. _____
7. _____
8. _____
8. _____
10. _____

Health

1. *Peace of mind*
2. *Independence*
3. _____
4. _____
5. _____

6. _____
7. _____
8. _____
8. _____
10. _____

1

You can learn how to close like the most successful producers do.

The 5 things to do before any close will work

No matter how convincing you are and how great our closing approaches are, you should not attempt to close until you know that the product is in their best interests, in other words, suitable. In addition, you will not close if:

- There is no need. (suitability)
- There are no real advantages to solving the need now.
- There is no money.
- There is no rapport between you and the prospect.
- You go after all of their money

Please review the last six months. Look for those appointments where you did not close. Visualize those interviews in your mind. Did you make sure that the first 4 points were addressed? Did you recommend that all of their CD money go into an annuity? Suggestion: give those prospects a call, meet with them again and do the following:

- Create a need.
- Share with them the benefits of solving that need now.
- Show them where they can find the money.
- Create that bond of trust.
- Go after some of their money

If you do each of the above, you will begin to experience a higher level of success as well as creating a more secure lifestyle for your clients and their families. (*Continued on next page*)

5 things to do before any close will work

1. Create a need

2. Share with them the benefits of solving that need now

3. Show them where they can find the money

4. Create that bond of trust

5. Go after some of their money

1 *You can learn how to close like the most successful producers do.*

(5 things to do before any close will work continued)

1 How To Create A Need

May we share a confession with you? For years and years, we sold the highest interest rate (and the lowest life and heath premium too) And, we did OK. Then, something happened. Interest rates for Certificates of Deposit—all of a sudden— became higher than the interest rates that annuity issuers were paying.

What did we do? We stopped selling the interest rate. Mrs. H. called it selling survival. We now call it very smart since we began asking people what they wanted. We listened. And, we began giving them what they wanted by asking,

- "Do you want to pay less income taxes?"

- "Do you want more money later?"

- "Do you want your family's lifestyle NOT to change for the worse if something unexpected occurs?"

- "Do you want your children to go to college?"

And, what happened when we went to a needs-based presentation? Sales went through the roof!

2 Share with them the benefits of solving that need now

We wish we could change how we describe ourselves on our business cards since we are a lot more than Registered Representatives, Insurance Professionals, and Presidents. We are Solutionists. We pinpoint problems and we formulate solutions. We ask people what they want and we help them get what they want by using our knowledge, experience, a legal pad and or cerebral, easy to use problem-solving software. *(Continued on next page)*

Ask
people
what they
want.

Listen.

Give them
what they
want.

1

You can learn how to close like the most successful producers do.

(5 things to do before any close will work continued)

#3 Show them where they can find the money

One statistic that we are NOT proud of is that well over 80% of all annuity business is a result of 1035 tax free exchanges, IRA Rollovers or IRA Transfers. In other words, we are NOT finding "new money". We are just moving the same money from one insurer to another.

Allow us to begin addressing this important issue by eventually asking you a question. Let's take a hypothetical couple who bought an annuity 10 years ago and over the last 10 years, they have seen 10 different insurance/investment professionals

Here is the question. How many times do you think that this hypothetical couple heard the insurance and investment professionals say that they had bought the wrong type of annuity or the old kind of annuity? Do you think they heard it 100% of the time? How do you think that couple feels about their annuity shopping skills? More importantly, how do you think they feel about meeting the next insurance/investment professional? Doesn't feel good about being reminded that you made a dumb decision, does it?

Find the money for them : Approach #1 and # 2

Please consider saying the words on the following page to the next annuity owner you meet. *(Continued on next page)*

Find the money for them: Approach #1

Annuity

"Ralph and Alice, 10 years ago, you made a wise decision when you bought an annuity.

Because of that wise decision that you made, you have paid less income taxes and now have more money. A very wise decision!

If you had needed money during the last 10 years, you had 4 different ways to get it: the 10% partial withdrawal, annuitization, the waiver of surrender charges for nursing home confinement, terminal illness, etc., or by surrendering and getting the annuity surrender value.

Ralph and Alice, 10 years ago, you made a wise decision.

Today, it is time again to make another wise decision. Let's take a look at some of the money that you have at the bank and let's again get some of that bank money accumulating on a tax-deferred basis with an annuity. Would you like to make another wise decision?

Find the money for them: Approach #2

Life and Health Insurance

In our book, *75 Secrets*, Secret 29 is titled A cup of coffee costs you $43,580 if you remain a spender. To make a long story short, we illustrate 4 examples of how some of us are unintentionally choosing coffee, cigarettes, soft drinks, over far more important issues such as being able to afford paying a Life, Health, and Annuity premium. Show them how they can redirect some of the money they spend on some products to an insurance premium that can be a lot more beneficial.

You can learn how to close like the most successful producers do.

(5 things to do before any close will work continued)

4 Create bond of trust and rapport

Unfortunately, there are 2 types of salespersons. The first type thinks they have a job and they measure success by how much money they made that day. So, when a prospect buys a product from them that pays them at GIGANTIC commission, they think they had a great day.

The second type of salesperson thinks they have a profession and they measure success by how much money they make in a career by helping a steadily-increasing clientele year after year.

The bottom line is that we owe our clients a pleasant buying experience for 2 reasons. Firstly and far more importantly, they deserve a great buying experience. Secondly, referrals and repeat business year after year often follow when we give them our best.

How do you create a bond of trust and rapport?

Make a nice first impression. Care about them more than yourself. Listen more than talk. Outline the products' disadvantages and advantages. Ascertain their tolerance for risk and their time horizon.

We have another homework assignment for you on the following page. Arguably, the most important homework assignment in the book since it will help you distinguish yourself above all others. *(Continued on next page)*

Please think of all of the insurance and investment professionals you know and list below all of the reasons why people should buy from *you* instead of them.

Important notes:

1. You cannot say anything bad about anyone.

2. You cannot mention the name of your insurance company or mutual fund since 400,000 other professionals can represent your insurance company and/or mutual fund as well.

3. This is a very important exercise on self-promotion. In other words, what makes you special.

1. *I return every call in the same day*
2. _____
3. _____
4. _____
5. _____
6. _____
7. _____
8. _____
8. _____
10. _____
11. _____
12. _____
13. _____
14. _____
15. _____

You can learn how to close like the most successful producers do.

(5 things to do before any close will work continued)

#5 Go after some of their money

Has a prospect ever told you that he/she had a $50,000, a $60,000, or a $70,000 Certificate of Deposit maturing the following week? And, did you ever go after all of it? Did you ever drive home with none of it? Begin helping your clients make wise financial decisions through diversification.

For example, you could never convince me to put all of my pension plan dollars into an annuity or any financial product for that matter. Why? Because investing all of my pension plan dollars into one plan is a very big decision. I would have to call my accountant and ask Tim for his opinion. I would have to ask Mrs. H. how she feels. But, if you were to go after 10%, 20%, or 30% of my pension plan dollars, I do feel comfortable making that decision.

Never go after your customers' all. When you do, you throw them into a state of indecision. But, even more importantly, you should never go after anyone's all because no one should put all of their dollars into any one thing, including the product you are recommending.

My Dad always said, "Never put all of your eggs in one basket." Did your Mom or Dad say the same thing? It is fair to assume that the Moms and Dads of your prospects, former clients, and clients told them too.

Tell a story of diversification to remove anxiety. More importantly, tell a story of diversification because no one should put all or most of their money in any one product or concept, including ours.

Did you ever go after all of their money and drive home with none of it?

My Dad always said, "Never put all of your eggs in one basket."

1 *You can learn how to close like the most successful producers do.*

The Best 12 Closes

We will soon give you the actual closing strategies and approaches that some of the most successful producers in America use. The key to each close is that you use the words that we bold. The words that follow the bolded words are benefits that we feel are great examples. However, the key to your success will be if you substitute our benefits with the benefits that you feel most passionate about. Use your passion. It is the easiest way to get to the next level of success.

#1 When would you like to?

This close is one of the best since it does not allow your prospect to procrastinate. Your prospects will say: "Today," "Immediately," "As soon as possible," "Right away," and "Now" when we use this proven close. What is this special close? It is simply:

"When would you like to stop paying income taxes?" or **"When would you like to** eliminate the taxes you're paying on your Social Security income?"

It is difficult to respond "later" to either of these two questions. You want say: "Now," "Right away," "Today," "Immediately," and "As soon as possible."

When they say, "now," you can say, "What is your Social Security number?" or "Do you want your statements mailed to your home or business address?"

On the following page, we have another homework assignment, where you can create your own **When would you like to** by adding the benefit that fuels your passion.

Homework Assignment

Please add the benefits to owning your products after you say, When would you like to?

1. **When would you like to** *start protecting yourself from living too long?*

2. **When would you like to** *start accumulating more money for retirement?*

3. **When would you like to** *stop paying income taxes?*

4. **When would you like to** *stop worrying about your money?*

5. **When would you like to** _____
   _____?

6. **When would you like to** _____
   _____?

7. **When would you like to** _____
   _____?

8. **When would you like to** _____
   _____?

9. **When would you like to** _____
   _____?

10. **When would you like to** _____
    _____?

11. **When would you like to** _____
    _____?

12. **When would you like to** _____
    _____?

13. **When would you like to** _____
    _____?

14. **When would you like to** _____
    _____?

15. **When would you like to** _____
    _____?

1 *You can learn how to close like the most successful producers do.*

#2 Do you see/Would you like/Is there any specific reason why you should not get started today?

Learning how to close is simple especially when you learn to use proven closes like asking 3 questions. It goes like this:

1. **Do you see...**
2. **Would you like...**
3. **Is there any specific reason why you should not get started today?**

For example:

1. **"Do you see** how this annuity will give you tax-deferred accumulation?"
2. **"Would you like** to have tax-deferred accumulation?"
3. **"Is there any specific reason why you shouldn't get started today?"**

Do you want something simpler? Simply replace the words in step 3 to "What is your Social Security number?" After all, the prospect did say "yes" to your second question. Notice the ingredients to the above.

1. Ask the prospect if they see the benefits of owning your product.
2. Ask them if they want those benefits.
3. Ask them for the order: "What is your Social Security number?"

You get the signature or the objection. You can have a good time with each.

Do you see how this closing approach can bring your prospects to closure? Would you like this approach to bring your prospects to closure? Is there a specific reason why you should not start using this approach today?

Homework Assignment

Do you see/Would you like/Is there any specific reason why you should not get started today?

Add the appropriate benefits to owning your product and practice using these 3 questions today, tonight, tomorrow in your car and then with every prospect this month.

1. a) **Do you see** *that the annuity can help you reduce the income taxes that you are paying on your Social Security income?*

   b) **Would you like** *the annuity to help you reduce the income taxes that you are paying on your Social Security income?*

   c) **Is there any specific reason why you should not get started today?**

2. a) **Do you see** _____?

   b) **Would you like**_____?

   c) **Is there any specific reason why you should not get started today?**

3. a) **Do you see** _____?

   b) **Would you like**_____?

   c) **Is there any specific reason why you should not get started today?**

1 *You can learn how to close like the most successful producers do.*

#3 The "Let's go ahead…"and #4 "I am going to assume" closes

We should use the following two interchangeable expressions at the beginning of a sentence before we begin to complete the application. For example, "**Let's go ahead** with it" and "**I am going to assume**." Following are some examples of how we would incorporate these two expressions into your dialogue at the beginning of every close. By the way, following each sentence, you would ask for their Social Security number.

#3 Let's go ahead

"**Let's go ahead** with diversifying your money a little more than it is now."

"**Let's go ahead** with protecting the people you love with the right amount of life insurance."

"**Let's go ahead** with this health insurance plan so that you are
doing what is right for you and your family."

#4 "I am going to assume…

- **I am going to assume** that you do not want to pay taxes on all of your interest earnings. (Now, ask for the Social Security number.)

- **I am going to assume** that you want your spouse to be the primary beneficiary of this life insurance policy." (Now, ask for the Social Security number.)

- **I am going to assume** that you want the benefits to increase 3% a year." (Now, ask for the Social Security number.)

Homework Assignment

The "Let's go ahead…"and "I am going to assume" closes

Add the appropriate benefits to owning your product.

1. **Lets go ahead** _____
   _____.

2. **Lets go ahead** _____
   _____.

3. **Lets go ahead** _____
   _____.

4. **Lets go ahead** _____
   _____.

5. **I am going to assume** _____
   _____.

6. **I am going to assume** _____
   _____.

7. **I am going to assume** _____
   _____.

8. **I am going to assume** _____
   _____.

1 *You can learn how to close like the most successful producers do.*

#5 "Let's talk..." and #6 "Can you think of a better way?"

Another effective way of bringing a prospect toward a decision which is in his or her best interest is by using "**Let's talk**". Following are some proven and successful closes which will help you and, more importantly, help them.

- **Let's talk** about who you would like your beneficiary to be.
- **Let's talk** about who you would like to own this policy.
- **Let's talk** about how you want your earnings credited.

The "better" close

Another effective close would be the "better" close. This close works so well since it will do one of two things. It will either bring a prospect toward the conclusion that he wants your product or it will allow you to get his objection surfaced. You win either way. With a yes, you get a signature. If they have a better way, you have their objection.

- **Can you think of a better way** to eliminate income taxes?
- **Can you think of a better way** to pay off your mortgage?
- **Can you think of a better way** to sidestep your partner's spouse working with you everyday"? (Buy-Sell insurance)
- **Can you think of a better way** to assure that there will be money for college?
- **Can you think of a better (and safer) way** for you to receive income for as long as you live?

Naturally, pause for a positive response and begin completing the application.

Homework Assignment

The "Let's talk…"and "Can you think of a better way?"

Following **Let's talk**, list a question you need answered on the application.

Following **Can you think of a better way**, list a benefit to owning your product.

1. **Lets talk** _____
   _____.

2. **Lets talk** _____
   _____.

3. **Lets talk** _____
   _____.

4. **Lets talk** _____
   _____

5. **Can you think of a better way** _____
   _____.

6. **Can you think of a better way** _____
   _____.

7. **Can you think of a better way** _____
   _____.

8. **Can you think of a better way** _____
   _____.

1 *You can learn how to close like the most successful producers do.*

#7 "I presume" close

Another effective, proven, successful closing technique is using the word "presume" whenever possible.

- "**I presume** that you would like to get started. What is your Social Security number?"

8 Trading Places

Just recently, I was speaking in West Palm Beach, Florida and a well-dressed investment professional approached me and shared the major problem he was having. In his 25 plus years in the profession, he was hearing "Sounds great, BUT let me think about it." more than ever.

I explained that more times than not, there is a hidden objection (or the 5 things we discussed on page 4 were not addressed).

He moved closer to me and asked for my suggestion. I offered the **Trading Places** close since it is one of the best ways to get the real objection surfaced. And, it goes something like this:

- Herbie,"If you were in my profession, and you wanted everyone you met to get this product that I have recommended for you, what additional benefits or features or changes would you ask the insurance company to make in order to get everyone to say "yes" to you?" (Pause for a response…if you talk first…both of you lose.)

If the prospect says he cannot think of anything special to add, your response should be:"I also feel this policy is perfect for you and your family. What is your Social Security number?" If they do give you something, then this "**Trading Places**" close did what it was supposed to do: It got the objection uncovered.

Homework Assignment
I presume...

Please add a benefit to owning your product.

1. **I presume** _you want tax control_ _____
_____.

2. **I presume**_____
_____.

3. **I presume**_____
_____.

4. **I presume**_____
_____.

5. **I presume**_____
_____.

6. **I presume**_____
_____.

7. **I presume**_____
_____.

8. **I presume**_____
_____.

9. **I presume**_____
_____.

10. **I presume**_____
_____.

① *You can learn how to close like the most successful producers do.*

#9 "Piece of Paper" close

This close is perfect for those who have heard your presentation before, but they just can't make a decision. No problem anymore because you can now say,

> "Mr. Jones, this" (holding an application in the air) "is an application for a single premium deferred annuity. During the next few moments, I will help you see that the annuity can potentially out–accumulate every other secure retirement vehicle. And, if you become totally convinced that the annuity can out–accumulate every other secure retirement vehicle, I will simply ask you to sign your name here on this application." (Point to signature line on application.) "However, if you are not totally convinced that the annuity can out–accumulate every other secure retirement vehicle, I will simply ask you which other secure retirement vehicle will out–accumulate an annuity. That is fair, isn't it?"

Have I made it crystal clear that I'll be asking for their signature? Yes, if they are totally convinced, otherwise, if they are not totally convinced, they must give you their objection.

That's what the piece of paper close does. It gets a "yes" or the "objection." Both are great because we can do something about each of them, can't we? With a yes, we complete the application. With an objection, we introduce new information.

#10 The "Print" close

The print close is much shorter and again you use the application. You simply say, looking the prospect in the eye:

> "Mr. Jones, I'm going to be printing your name and address on this application which acknowledges that you want to protect the people you love. You do want to protect the people you love, don't you?"

With a "yes," we complete the application. With an objection, we introduce new information.

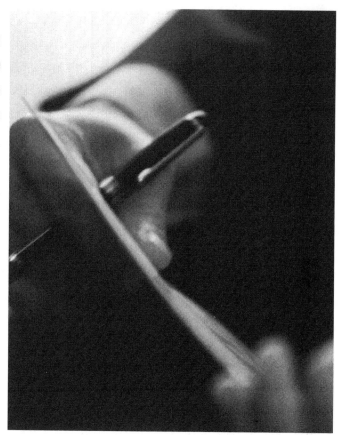

You can learn how to close like the most successful producers do.

#11 Choice closes that work well

We all like choices, don't we? I know that I do. Do you? Anyway, I have included a list of choices you can now give to your prospects and clients. If you use these, this year will be very special.

1. Do you want your premiums levels for 5 or 10 years?
2. Do you want your benefits to increase at 3% or remain level?
3. Do you want your insurance to decrease like your mortgage or remain level?
4. Do you want to pay taxes now or later?
5. Do you want statements mailed to your home or business address?
6. Do you want a 1 year or 5 year interest rate?
7. Do you want to own the annuity or do you want to own it jointly with your spouse?
8. Do you want a lower interest rate with a smaller penalty period or a higher rate with a longer surrender charge period?

You will soon think that we have saved the best close for last. In actuality, the source for this secret has been my memory plus one of our former books, *The Encyclopedia To Annuity Success*, but with recent experiences gently weaved into the meat of the topic, Closing. However, I just—suddenly and embarrassingly—realized that the BEST CLOSE of all time was missing from our book and recent memory too.

What is the BEST CLOSE of all time? Allow me to tell you a story first. In the 1990's , we had written a book titled The *Encyclopedia to Annuity Selling*. It was a big 6 pound $365 book that 22,000 financial professionals now have on their bookshelves. Retired professionals, hopefully, still have it in their basement.

From 1990-1997, we traveled to 5 cities every week and asked large and small audiences if they wanted to own the book. We also mailed 2,000 mailers a day. You may have seen it. It was titled "Who are you seeing next week that has $10,000 in the bank?" The mailer had a BIG picture of the book and BIG words at the bottom that said, call 1-800-800-SALE if you want a FREE brochure. When you called, we had an entire team of consultants who would take down your mailing address and begin to share the benefits of owning the book that day instead of next week.

#11 Choice closes that work well continued)

If everyone was on the phone and if I were not real, real busy, I would take the call. Some of the nicest relationships were started on those types of calls. But, one day at 5:30 AM (pacific), a financial professional from Boston called. I answered the phone and the first thing he did was to explain his predicament. He was in a slump. A one year slump. And, as the conversation continued, I realized that of ALL financial professionals I had spoken to, this guy needed our book more than anyone else. He did not know how to overcome objections about surrender charges or safety. He did not know how to find annuity prospects He did not know our now famous 5 Benefit annuity presentation.

Of ALL people I had ever spoken to, he needed our book more than anyone else. In fact, I was sure that he would ask me to stop my presentation so he could order the book. Surprisingly, he allowed me to finish. So, when I finished, I paused and waited for him to say he wanted the book shipped that day. I waited and waited. Finally, I said "Would you like me to send you the brochure? He said yes, and, of course, we sent him the brochure.

The next day, I was speaking in San Diego to a major stock brokerage firm and ironically, my topic was How To Close. During the presentation, I said to myself, "You hypocrite Harris, how dare you talk about closing after that phone call yesterday from Boston. After the presentation, I ran to my car, sped to my office, ran up two floors of steps, sat at my desk, and asked my ENTIRE organization (of 5 people) to sit around my desk. I embarrassingly told them what happened over the phone the day before and I asked them to write down the following words and to say those words at the end of every call.

And what were those words? "Well, would you like to go ahead with it?" Friends, our sales nearly doubled the following year for us. Industry statistics show that we only ask for the order 50% of the time. Beginning today, please ask for the order 100% *of the time. And the easiest softest way to close is to say "Well, would you like to go ahead with it?

Ask for the order 100% of the time—assuming the annuity is suitable for them.

1 *You can learn how to close like the most successful producers do.*

Summary: In this secret, you learned

- The definition of a great closer
- One of the obstacles we face: Acting
- The 5 things to do before any close will work
- How to create a need
- The benefits of solving that need now
- Where they can find the money
- The importance of creating a bond of trust and rapport
- How to create a bond of trust and rapport
- To go after some of their money
- The Best 12 Closes
  - When would you like to
  - Do you see/Would you like/Is there any specific reason why you should not get started today?
  - Let's go ahead
  - I am going to assume…
  - Let's talk
  - The "better" close
  - Can you think of a better way
  - I presume
  - Trading Places
  - Pieces of Paper
  - Print
  - Well, would you like to go ahead with it?

secret **2**

You can use the phone like a pro to prospect, make appointments, and sell.

The phone! We use it to prospect, to make appointments, and to present. We use the phone to inform and persuade. We use the phone to call people we already know, people we don't know yet, and we even use the phone to call people that sadly we will never know. In this secret, you will learn how to maximize the real power behind the phone. Unquestionably, if you follow this secret carefully and follow each and every suggestion, you will acquire a level of success you never thought possible.

2 *You can use the phone like a pro to prospect, make appointments, and sell.*

What you will soon learn?

You'll soon learn the six things you need to succeed over the phone. How to overcome call reluctance. The 5 steps to follow before writing a phone script and how to write a telephone script for any product. You will learn how to overcome almost any phone objection, the smartest ways to reduce telephone tag, and proven best ways to deal with your prospect's "protective" administrative assistant.

Examining how you feel about your product

While we should spend 60% of our time with our clients and referrals, we must continuously fill our pipeline with new prospects and using the phone is one of the ways. Pessimists refer to this as cold-calling since pessimists wake up in the morning saying, *"Well, today is the day that I have to make 100 cold calls."* If you wake up in the morning saying you have to make 100 cold calls, you will have 100 cold calls. On the other hand, if you wake up in the morning saying, *"Well, today is the day that I will be paid $1,250 to ask 100 people if they would like me to help them think about their money."* Then, you will have made 100 calls that will generate results.

On the opposite page, we have an important homework assignment for you to do. Why is it important? After doing the assignment, you will have an important page to read before you make any future cold call. The assignment is also important since we owe it to our family to be the best that we can be in this profession. And, you are one page away from having the perfect attitude whenever a phone is in your hand.

Homework Assignment
Please list 10 ways you help people. After completing this assignment, please read it in its entirety before making any future cold calls and even calls to your current prospects, former clients, referrals, and clients.

Well, today is the day that I will be paid $1,250 to ask 100 people if they would like me to help them

1. *Think about their money on a regular basis.*
2. _____
3. _____
4. _____
5. _____
6. _____
7. _____
8. _____
8. _____
10. _____
11. _____
12. _____
13. _____
14. _____
15. _____

2 *You can use the phone like a pro to prospect, make appointments, and sell.*

The 6 things you need to do to succeed over the phone

Reaching out to new prospects, current prospects, former clients, referrals, and existing clients is extremely inexpensive, especially after you realize what it can do for you. What do you need to succeed over the phone? All you need are these six things:

1. Belief in your product.

2. A desire to help people.

3. The right phone script.

4. Good phone skills.

5. The right names to call.

6. A pre-arranged, designated time to call people.

Call Reluctance

Now, please answer this question: Why do 20% of any sales force usually make 80% of all sales? Answer! They call more people. Why don't they ever encounter call reluctance? They do but they know how to lessen call reluctance. What is call reluctance? Call reluctance is not picking up the phone enough times. Symptoms of call reluctance are excuses for not calling people such as waiting for a better time to call or waiting for a better phone script. The effect of call reluctance is always the same: fewer sales.

Here are some of the symptoms of this "disease," which we all, at one point or another, encounter at least once or twice a year.

Call reluctance symptom No. 1

Have you ever picked up the telephone, then put it down because it was not the best time to call. This reasoning is almost comical. How do you know when the best time to call is? The next time you hear that little monster inside of you saying, "Now is not the best time." immediately pick up the phone. (assuming it is before 8:00 PM)

(Continued on page ?)

(Call reluctance continued)

Call reluctance symptom No. 2

How many times have you thought, "If I call now, I might sound too aggressive. I just met with him last week." Let's examine this statement. We might be too aggressive if we are trying to sell him something that he did not need. But, that's not what you're doing. You are selling peace of mind, protection, dignity. You are selling a product which allows for more dollars at retirement and a more enjoyable life.

Call reluctance symptom No. 3

Have you ever postponed "calling out" because you thought, "I need a better telephone script."The real truth of the matter is that these symptoms are merely excuses. We are only kidding ourselves. We must begin calling people today.

"The worst telephone script used every day is far better than the best telephone script used once a week."

The 4 things to do to cure call-reluctance

First, we must learn to recognize call reluctance. We must say to ourselves, "Yes, I am experiencing call reluctance."

Second, we must recognize the *humor* in call reluctance. Visualize how we look when we create excuses for not picking up the phone. Imagine yourself being observed by your associates, by your children, and by your spouse. You are sitting behind your desk, shuffling papers, frequently calling home, making trips to the rest room, checking your email, chatting with others in your office, checking LinkedIn and Facebook and Tweeting. You are doing just about everything possible to avoid picking up that phone and asking people if they would like to be seen. Solution? Read that homework assignment you did on page 31 that stated the 15 ways you help people. *(Continued on next page)*

2 *You can use the phone like a pro to prospect, make appointments, and sell.*

(*The 4 things to do to cure call-reluctance continued*)

How to cure call reluctance…

Third, let's review some of the ways people benefit by meeting with you and let's see how many of these were on your list.

1. Money can be provided when it is needed the most: at disability, retirement, and death.
2. Money for emergencies and for opportunities.
3. Less income taxes.
4. A more comfortable lifestyle.
5. Children can go to college.
6. Mortgages can be paid in full if "it" happens.
7. Surviving spouses have enough money at the end of every month.

After reviewing all of the benefits we can provide to people, pick up the phone. Who should you call first? Anyone. The 40 people who received your letter this week. The 60 business owners you exchanged business cards with last week. The qualified referrals that you collected. Any clients of yours who may need a policy review.

Will you feel nervous during the initial phone calls? Of course. Feeling nervous is normal. Call reluctance is normal. However, reluctance will diminish with every phone call you make and you will feel more comfortable in time. Fortunately, eliminating call reluctance is easy. Just act by picking up the phone and asking people if they would like to be seen and helped. (*Continued on next page*)

(Call reluctance continued)

3 easy-to-follow steps to curing Call Reluctance

The next call reluctance cure has two easy-to-follow steps.

Just visualize the following two things:

1. Visualize a person saying to you "Don't call me again."

2. Visualize a person asking you a question to which you do not know the answer.

Now, let's learn what you will say if you hear these things.

1. If a person strongly says that he or she does not want you to call them again, say: "I am sorry for calling you at an inconvenient time. I will not call you again. Have a nice day."

2. If asked a question that you do not know the answer to, say:
   "That's a good question. Rather than give you a partial answer, allow me to research that further, and when we get together, I will be able to give that answer to you. Where would be the best place for us to get together. Your place, my office, or at a coffee shop nearby?"

You have now visualized 2 of the worst things that may happen to you when you call people. And, you now know what to say if one of those things happens. Now, what else is there to worry about? Nothing! Please pick up the phone and begin calling almost anyone.

2 *You can use the phone like a pro to prospect, make appointments, and sell.*

Should we give them 2 choices or 3 choices:

"Would Monday be good or is Tuesday better?" Or "Where would be the best place for us to get together for 15 minutes? Your place, my office, or at a coffee shop nearby?"

Before we continue, let's address a very important issue. From almost the beginning of time, a sales professional was taught to give only 2 choices to a prospect. Hence, "Would Monday be good or is Tuesday better?"

However, times have changed. The consumers get more phone calls now than ever before. Arguably, they are less receptive now to change and more suspicious of whether the product is in their best interests.

When they get a phone call from someone they do not know, do you think there are experiencing any anxiety? Of course, they are. Therefore, we must learn, master, and refine how to reduce their anxiety. Why? Because they only win after they get together with you. It is only after they say "Yes" to you that they pay less taxes, accumulate more money, protect the people they love, and have dignity during retirement.

How do we reduce anxiety for them? Make it easy for them to meet you. Suggest a 15 minute initial meeting. Meet them at a nearby coffee shop. Suggest that they bring a friend, neighbor or one of their adult children. Are there any better places to meet than at coffee shop? How about a library? Museum? In my circle, I do not know too many who would refuse an ice cream cone at a nearby ice cream parlor during the spring, summer, and fall.

The 5 important steps to follow before writing your phone script

1. You should first establish goals and determine what you would like to achieve.

    1. Are you trying to sell your products over the phone?

    2. Are you trying to schedule an appointment?

    3. Are you trying to get permission to send them a brochure?

2. You should know how much time, which hours of the day, and which day(s) you will be devoting strictly to making phone calls.

    A successful telephone campaign requires discipline and structure.

3. You must know who you are calling. When you rent names from a mailing list broker, you may have some extra information about the people you are calling (occupation, length of residence, age, or home value). If you are calling your current customers and referrals, you will have more information about them.

4. You should first jot down all the benefits that people acquire by owning your product. Focus on the benefits and not the features.

5. Your script should have no more than 7 sentences. If the purpose of your call is to schedule an appointment or mail a brochure, then your script should be shorter and take approximately 30 seconds, from beginning to completion, to recite.

2 *You can use the phone like a pro to prospect, make appointments, and sell.*

Dissecting the ideal phone script into 4 parts

1. The introduction

   Mr. Jones, I hope this is this a good time to talk. (no pause)

2. The explanatory section

   I work with many (*say your specialty market such as small business owners or young married couples* or those receiving Social Security) and the reason I am calling is that I would like to stop by, shake hands with you, and drop off some information on how we (*say how you help that specialty market*).

   Example 1: I work with many *small business owners* and the reason I am calling is that I would like to stop by, shake hands with you, and drop off some information on how we help *small business owners* such as yourself accumulate more money for retirement.

   Example 2: I work with many *young married couples* and the reason I am calling is that I would like to stop by, shake hands with you, and drop off some information on how we help *young married couples* insure their mortgage.

3. The bridge

   I know that you would like to (repeat the benefit such as accumulate more money or insure their mortgage) wouldn't you? (no pause)

4. The close

   Where would be the best place for us to get together for 15 minutes? Your place, my office, or at a coffee shop nearby?

Summary of the 4 things to do during every phone call.

   1. Introduction
   2. Give them the reason for your call.
   3. State your benefit using a "wouldn't you?" question.
   4. Give them a choice of where to meet and the risk of meeting you. (15 minutes of their time)

On the following page, we have another homework assignment where you can list all of your specialty markets and how you help them.

Homework Assignment

Please identify your specialty markets and how you help them.

1. I work with many *small business owners* and the reason I am calling is that I would like to stop by, shake hands with you, and drop off some information on how we help *small business owners* such as yourself accumulate more money for retirement.

2. I work with many *young married couples* and the reason I am calling is that I would like to stop by, shake hands with you, and drop off some information on how we help *young married couples* insure their mortgage.

3. I work with many _____ and the reason I am calling is that I would like to stop by, shake hands with you, and drop off some information on how we help (specialty market and how you help them) _____

   _____.

4. I work with many _____ and the reason I am calling is that I would like to stop by, shake hands with you, and drop off some information on how we help (specialty market and how you help them) _____

   _____.

5. I work with many _____ and the reason I am calling is that I would like to stop by, shake hands with you, and drop off some information on how we help (specialty market and how you help them) _____

   _____.

6. I work with many _____ and the reason I am calling is that I would like to stop by, shake hands with you, and drop off some information on how we help (specialty market and how you help them) _____

   _____.

2 *You can use the phone like a pro to prospect, make appointments, and sell.*

---

13 additional phone tips

1. Be polite.

2. We should always smile during the introduction and keep that smile on your voice.

3. Assume that they are going to say yes before, during, and at the end of your phone call.

4. When clients talk, do not interrupt them. We should listen to every word they say. Listen carefully. Remember, a true professional is also a great listener.

5. If they are not interested, ask them if you could call them later when things might be a little better. If they say OK, send them a nice note that day expressing that you enjoyed talking to them and that you look forward to calling them in 30 days. Fifteen days later, send them another note like "I thought this article about Social Security would be of interest to you. I look forward to calling you in 15 days". On the 30th day, you MUST call them. Why? You said you would. Our greatest asset is our word.

   If they do not want you to call back, end the conversation with excellent phone etiquette by being positive and upbeat. We should thank them for their time and extend to them a very nice day.

6. Never argue or debate any issue with a caller.

7. After using a phone script for about 10 to 14 hours, you will be in a position to know its effectiveness.

8. We should practice our telephone script with colleagues and family members.

9. We should write down the script in an outline form so that our tone will be very conversational. Do not use a phone script verbatim.

10. We should never put the receiver down. We should always keep the phone in our hand between phone calls.

11. During a cold call, you should never ask a question if you do not know the answer. For example, some questions you should not ask during a cold call might be:

    Is this a good time to talk?

    How are you feeling?

    Now when you call me and I return the phone call, the first thing I will say to you is "Is this a good time to talk?" Said differently, when making a call to an associate, client, referral, always show good phone etiquette by asking" Is this a good time to talk?" But do not ask a question if you do not know the answer when making a cold call.

12. Call standing up. I have never never made an important phone call sitting down. Oh, I have made plenty of calls sitting down but I did not think they were important. Since the difference between keeping a prospect a prospect and converting a prospect into a client can be measured in thousands of dollars, call standing up for the best delivery.

13. Do not use your cell phone unless the cell phone is your only choice. Why? You can never change anyone's first impression of you and poor audio quality and an unintentional hang-up does not make a good impression.

2 *You can use the phone like a pro to prospect, make appointments, and sell.*

The 10 most frequently used phone objections

A true professional is a person who is prepared for every possible objection. Let's now discuss how to overcome phone objections using special proven approaches. Will it be easy to prepare for phone objections? Yes, prospects are saying the same things they have been saying for the last three decades. The objections have not changed. But, we have. We now know what to say when they say:

> I have all the insurance that I want.
>
> I'm too busy.
>
> I can do better with my money!
>
> I am insurance poor.
>
> I don't have any money.
>
> I am happy with my agent.
>
> I don't have enough time.
>
> I have a friend in the business.
>
> I am all taken care of.
>
> I would like to talk it over with my spouse.

A true professional is a person who is prepared for every objective. And, as sales professionals, we must learn how to overcome these phone objections. Fortunately, this is easy to learn.

The easiest ways to overcome almost any objection

Ninety percent of all phone objections can be addressed using the next two approaches. You'll notice that we are not giving much credence to their objection since we are saying the same thing regardless of their objection. Most phone objections are brush-offs, artificial objections. Needless to say, if you hear a specific genuine objection, then address that objection head-on with respect.

The first way to overcome almost any phone objection is to show prospects that they will benefit by seeing you because of their objection.

For example, when you hear an objection, you should always say the same thing.

"I can appreciate how you feel. However the people who benefit the most from my services are people who" (repeat their objection).

"Where would be the best place for us to get together for 15 minutes? Your place, my office, or at a coffee shop nearby?"

Let's see how the approach works by giving four examples.

Their objection

I already own annuities.

Your response

"I can appreciate how you feel. However, people who often benefit the most from my services are people who already own annuities." (then the best place to meet for 15 minutes close) (Continued on next page)

2 *You can use the phone like a pro to prospect, make appointments, and sell.*

(The first way to overcome almost any phone objection Continued)

Their objection

I am insurance poor.

Your response

"I can appreciate how you feel. However people who often benefit the most from my services are people who feel that they are insurance poor." (then the best place to meet for 15 minutes close)

Their objection

I would like to discuss it with my wife/husband.

Your response

"I can appreciate how you feel. However the people who often benefit the most from my services are people who would like to discuss things over with their spouse." (then the best place to meet for 15 minutes close)

Their objection

I am happy with my agent.

Your response

"I can appreciate how you feel. However the people who often benefit the most from my services are people who are happy with their agent." (then the best place to meet for 15 minutes close)

Brush-Off Objection Summary

1. Appreciate their objection.

2. Point out to the prospect that they will benefit more from your services because of their objection.

3. Illustrate the risk of the appointment. In other words, 15 minutes of their time or a handshake.

4. Close for the appointment again by giving them a choice close.

The second way to overcome any phone objection is to use the words feel, felt, and found "by reversing their brush-off objection."

For example, whenever you hear an objection, you should always say the same thing.

"I can appreciate how you feel. Many of my clients felt that same way. However, they have found that (Reverse their objection) after they saw what I could do for them. Where would be the more convenient place to meet for 15 minutes together? Your place, my place or at a coffee shop nearby."

Let's see how this approach works by giving six examples.

Their objection	Your response
I am insurance poor.	"I can appreciate how you feel. Many of my clients felt the same way. However, they found that they were not insurance poor after they saw what I could do for them." (the convenient place close)

Their objection	Your response
I never tie my money up for longer than a year.	"I can appreciate you feel. Many of my clients felt the same way. However, they found that they were not tying up their money after they saw what I could do for them." (the convenient place close)

2 *You can use the phone like a pro to prospect, make appointments, and sell.*

Their objection	Your response
I can do better with my money.	"I can appreciate how you feel. Many of my clients felt the same way. However, they found that they couldn't do better with their money after they saw what I could do for them." (the convenient place close)

Their objection	Your response
Contact me later.	"I can appreciate how you feel. Many of my clients felt the same way. However, they found that getting together now had been a good idea after they saw what I could do for them." (the convenient place close)

Their objection	Your response
I would like to discuss it with my spouse.	"I can appreciate how you feel. Many of my clients felt the same way. However, they found that they would only have something to discuss with their spouse after they saw what I could do for them." (the convenient place close)

Important note:

When overcoming phone objections, we should not use approach number 1 on some days and approach number 2 on others. We should stick with one strategy whenever possible. Ted Williams didn't change his batting stance at every time at bat. He stuck with the same stance. So should we.

How to overcome the objection "Send me a brochure first"

We need only two approaches to address and overcome 9,998 "brush-off" objections. However, there are unique instances when our two approaches will not work. Do you remember in school when your English teacher reviewed subject/verb agreements and there were some exceptions to the rule? Well, "Can you send me a brochure first?" requires an exception. In fact, use either one of these two approaches the next time you hear, "Can you send me a brochure first?"

1. "Mr. Jones, I am the brochure." (A smile should be in your voice.)

2. "Mr. Jones, I would like to send you a brochure. However, my insurance license allows me to represent 2,000 insurance companies and my securities license allows me to recommend 2,000 mutual funds and 2,000 different corporations on the New York Stock Exchange. I could mail you 6,000 brochures, prospectuses, and annual reports, but you only want one and I'll only know the best one to leave with you after we spend 15 minutes together."(the convenient place close)

How to overcome the objection "What is this all about?"

Occasionally, we will hear an objection, "What is this all about?" or "What do you do for a living?" When we hear that objection, we should say:

> "I provide individuals, families, and businesses with special types of insurance. Insurance against inflation. Insurance against disability. Insurance against your family not being able to pay the mortgage." (the convenient place close)

2 *You can use the phone like a pro to prospect, make appointments, and sell.*

The 5 ways to reduce telephone tag

A recent survey reported that close to three years of one's lifetime will be spent in "telephone tag." Three years of unproductive time. Three years of not selling, three years of not asking for the order, and three years of not doing anything positive for ourselves, our family, or for our customers and their families.

Telephone tag costs the average sales professional thousands of dollars each year.

Can we eliminate telephone tag? No, we really cannot eliminate telephone tag. However, we can reduce it by using the following phone skills.

Ask specifically when the person you are calling will be returning.

Ask specifically if the person will be very busy when he returns and would there be a more convenient time for you to call back.

If the person you are trying to reach is on another line, ask if you can be put on hold.

Ask to be transferred to the person's voice mail if you have already made repeated attempts.

There is a time to quit. Do not be too persistent. Do not leave your name after you have done so two times in one week. After you have tried to contact a person several times, send a letter.

The 4 things to do in order to get past the prospect's protective administrative assistant

The administrative assistant is there to "protect" the boss. Here are some ways to effectively deal with an administrative assistant.

1. We should always stay in control of the conversation.

2. We should ask the questions.

3. We should make the recommendations.

4. We should start the call the right way, "This is Bill Harris with W.V.H., Inc., please put me through to Paul, thank you." (Do not pause after the prospect's name.) This is much more effective than saying to the secretary, "Is Mr. Jones there?"

5. We should anticipate the objections that we will be hearing and be ready with a response.

2 *You can use the phone like a pro to prospect, make appointments, and sell.*

We have listed below a few of the objections we may hear when speaking with administrative assistant and what our response would be.

The 4 phone objections from the administrative assistant.

Objection	Your response
What is this all about?	"I would like Paul's opinion. Thank you. (If asked, "Opinion on what?") The new ways he can make large tax-deductible contributions for the corporation's employees' retirement. Please put me through. Thank you."
May I help you?	(smile in voice) "No, thank you. I need Paul's opinion. Please put me through. Thank you."
He is busy.	"When would be a more convenient time to talk with him? Would this afternoon at 4:00 p.m. be good, or would tomorrow morning be better?" (Try to book a telephone appointment.)
Can I have your telephone number?	"Thank you anyway. When would be a more convenient time for me to give him a call back? Would this afternoon be good, or would tomorrow morning be better?"

Whenever possible, obtain the administrative assistant's first name and use it, but only once or twice during the conversation. Be personal. The administrative assistant can be an asset. Remember, both of you want what's best for "Paul".

Summary: In this secret, you learned

Secret 8
gives you
2 proven
popular
phone
scripts
plus 8 new
scripts.

- The 6 things you need to succeed over the phone
- How to examine how you feel about your product
- How to spot the 3 symptoms of call reluctance early
- How to cure call reluctance
- 5 important steps to follow before writing your phone script
- 4 parts to an ideal phone script
- The 4 things to do during every phone call
- 13 additional phone tips
- The easiest ways to overcome almost any objection
- How to allow their objections to become their solutions
- How to overcome the objection "Send me a brochure first."
- How to overcome the objection "What is this all about?"
- 5 ways to reduce telephone tag
- 4 things to do in order to get past the prospect's protective administrative assistant

2 *You can use the phone like a pro to prospect, make appointments, and sell.*

Phone Quiz

1. To succeed over the phone, you need everything Except

   a) belief in your product
   b) a desire to help people
   c) good phone skills
   d) a voice for radio

2. The part of a phone script where we describe your specialty market and how you help people is called

   a) introduction
   b) explanatory section
   c) close

3. Good phone tips would be

   a) being polite
   b) assume that they will say yes
   c) do not argue
   d) all of the above

Answers: 1. d 2. b 3. d

3

You can get referrals consistently.

Without a doubt, the number of qualified referrals we get every day will have more of an impact on our sales careers than any other phase of selling. If you hate to ask for referrals, don't worry. If you often leave interviews without enough referrals, don't worry. If you do not have a Referral System, don't worry. You should only worry if you think you don't need referrals to get you to that higher level of selling success.

3 *You can get referrals consistently.*

Please answer these questions for me: Who do you know who needs business cards? Who do you know who wants a new den? You probably didn't think of too many people, did you? Our clients don't think of too many prospects either if we ask for referrals the wrong way. We will stop asking "Who do you know that might be interested in an annuity? " or "Mr. Jones, who do you know who (add your favorite one-liner)?"

Their response is always the same . . . a blank stare followed by the words, "I can't think of anyone." That is why we need a new Referral System. The present one is not working. However, our Referral System will work for you.

Why will you like our Referral System? You won't have to ask clients for the names of referrals like you once did ever again. Yet you will leave each interview, annual review and service call with almost too many referrals. This is all possible when you use our Referral Folder and Referral System the right way.

What else do you need? Besides the folder, you need the right attitude, you need to use any one of seven proven referral-creating approaches, and you need to turn the page.

A referral attitude

How do you currently feel about referrals? Have you ever felt that asking for referrals was condescending? Do you feel it is awkward sometimes to ask a client for additional prospects? These feelings can damage your career. If you really want to acquire a higher level of success—and we know you do—you must change your attitude!

If you are in the business market, you want your clients to respect you. How does the president of any sales firm feel about you if he sees you walking away without asking for referrals? Successful salespeople like to do business with other successful salespeople. We do, don't you?

One of the easiest ways to change our attitude about asking for referrals is to begin reflecting on what we and our product can do for these referrals when we get together with them.

- They can begin to diversify.
- They can receive guidance from qualified money managers.
- They can defer current taxes on their investment earnings.
- They can adjust their portfolio as their needs change.
- They can slash health care costs
- They protect the people that they love with life insurance.

Simply put, we are helping others help the people they love if they die too soon or if they live too long or if they get sick or hurt.

Making a sale without acquiring qualified referrals is only one-half of a sale, an incomplete sale, a partial sale. A sale without a referral is short-term success resulting in a long-term problem. However, a sale with referrals is a career.

> *A sale without a referral is short-term success resulting in a long-term problem. However, a sale with referrals is a career.*

3 *You can get referrals consistently.*

We are paid in two ways and our clients and prospects should understand this. First, we are paid a commission to service the products we sell. We are paid this commission by the insurance company which issues the product that we sell and service. The second form of compensation we receive is paid to us by our client. However, we are not paid in dollars but rather in referrals.

Here is an example of what we could tell each of our prospects at the beginning of every sales interview regarding the ways we are compensated:

"I receive two types of compensation. First, I get paid from the companies that I have agreed to represent. They pay me for processing their applications, for describing how their product works, and for my willingness to be there whenever clients need me, mornings, afternoons, and evenings, seven days a week, 365 days a year.

My second form of compensation comes from you. If you feel that I was professional and that I helped you make a wise decision, I would like you to tell people that you are my client. This will allow me to help those people just as I helped you. That sounds fair, doesn't it?"

Telling a prospective client in the very beginning that you will be asking for referrals later is an important step. However, how we begin compiling qualified referrals is a more important step.

In the following pages, we unveil proven ways of obtaining qualified referrals. You'll notice that we do not rely on "Who do you know that might be interested in my product or services?"

Interested? If so, please turn the page to learn how to meet neighbors of your clients, people who work with your clients, people who are in the same profession as your clients, and other people your clients know.

Said differently, turn the page if you want the most professional way to ask for referrals and the easiest way to file all of the referrals in one place.

3 *You can get referrals consistently.*

The Referral Folder

As you will soon see, our Referral Folder, asking the right questions, and Reverse Directories become your easiest way for you to get referrals consistently. As you are aware, a Reverse Directory is like a telephone book in reverse since it lists names based upon the street address. You can use a Reverse Directory at your local library. It is typically chained to a leg of the table. Or, you can google the phrase "Reverse Directory" on your computer and find hundreds of online Reverse Directories. Some are free. Make sure that the terms of usage with the online Reverse Directory allows you to use it for prospecting purposes.

Our
Referral
Folder

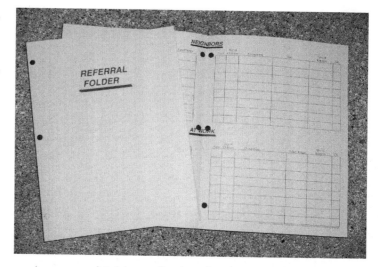

- •
- •
- •
- •
- •
- •

• • • gives you a highly professional way to ask for referrals and the easiest way to file all of the referrals in one place.

3 *You can get referrals consistently.*

On the opposite page, we show the Neighbors section of our special Referral Folder. Special since this folder can single-handedly change your life.

How do you use the Referral Folder? Prior to every policy delivery, service call, and annual review, go online, google the phrase reverse directory, find your favorite one, and enter the street address of the client that you are seeing later that day. Click on the search button and watch the names and the telephone numbers of all of your client's neighbors appear.

Now take out your Referral Folder or legal pad and start writing down the last name (not the first name), street address, and telephone number for the 8 neighbors who live closest to your client.

At the end of your appointment with your client say,

> "I was planning on calling these people listed here. (Point to the 8 names already written down in your folder.) I am sure that you know some of these people. Which ones do you know on a first-name basis?

Begin with the first name,

> What are Mr. & Mrs. Phillips first-name?

Begin with the first name,

Then get the neighbor's first name and write it down. Move on to the second name. Now after reviewing each of the 8 names, return to the first name.

> Ask for their approximate ages. Their occupations.
> If you wish, ask them the ages of their children.
> Favorite sports team.

Now, continue on with the others in the same way. After you finish getting all of the information, ask the $64,000 question: "If I were to call them, you wouldn't mind if I mentioned that you were my client, would you?" Then make a check mark under OK in your folder. Naturally, only call those names who are not on the DO NOT CALL LIST. We'll use a different strategy with those DNC names.

NEIGHBORS

Name	Address	Phone	First Name
1. Phillips	10211 Main Street, USA	555-1112	
2. Jones	10212 Main Street, USA	555-1113	
3. Menez	10213 Main Street, USA	555-1114	
4. Scolnick	10214 Main Street, USA	555-1115	
5. Woods	10215 Main Street, USA	555-1116	
6. Lemmo	10216 Main Street, USA	555-1117	
7. O'Neil	10217 Main Street, USA	555-1118	
8. Payne	10218 Main Street, USA	555-1119	

	Ages	Age of Children	Occupation	Salary Range	Special Interests	OK
1.						
2.						
3.						
4.						
5.						
6.						
7.						
8.						

3 *You can get referrals consistently.*

For clients in management

When you are with a client who is in management, it is often an excellent idea for you to solicit names of other professionals who report to your client. Again using the Referral Folder on the opposite page.

"Joe, who are the people at work who report to you?"

Again ask permission for you to mention that they are your client.

When you call these referrals, they are often flattered that their boss or supervisor thought enough of them to give you their names.

After you have compiled these names, begin collecting names of referrals who are in the same salary range as your client.

"Who is in the office next to you at work? Who is in the office across the hall? At the last meeting, what other executives were in the room with you?"

AT WORK : People Who Report To You

	First Name	Last Name	Position	Age	OK
1.					
2.					
3.					
4.					
5.					
6.					
7.					
8.					

AT WORK : Colleagues

	First Name	Last Name	Title	Age	OK
1.					
2.					
3.					
4.					
5.					
6.					
7.					
8.					

3 *You can get referrals consistently.*

The philosophy behind this referral approach

Notice what we are now doing. We are no longer asking clients "Who do you know who might be interested in an annuity or in life or health insurance?" We are selecting the name or type of referral in advance. We are just asking clients for the first names of their neighbors, the names of those they work with, and permission to say that they are your client. Before, we were allowing our clients to control who our future clients were going to be. Now we control our destiny We now know who we want as clients, people whom your client is most apt to know. Instead of saying, "Who do you know?" you are now asking the right questions like:

> "I was planning on calling these people next week. I'm sure that you know some of these people. Do you know Mr. or Mrs. Phillips?"

> or "Which people report to you?"

> or "Who is in the office next to you?"

In the Professional Section of the Referral Folder, you again select who you want as a client and simply ask your client if they know that person you want as a client. Since doctors know doctors, if you were delivering a policy to a doctor, you would say " I was planning to call these 10 cardiologists. Which ones do you know on a first name basis? Do you know Dr. Botello? What about Dr. Anderson? Then, after reviewing all 10 names, go back and get more info like approximate age, etc. Then ,the $64,000 question comes last. "When I call them , you would not mind if I mentioned that you were my client, would you?

Use the Professional Section of your Referral Folder to get the first names of prospective clients you want as clients who are in the same profession as your client.

In the Questions To Ask section of the Referral Folder, you get more sales-creating, career-enhancing questions to ask. Most importantly, you ask the questions that you feel like asking. You are a professional and you can feel which questions make the most sense to ask. After all, you are seeing your clients again and you do NOT need one zillion referrals from them right away.

PROFESSIONALS

First Name	Last Name	Age	OK
Dr. James	Botello		
Dr. Helen	Anderson		
Dr. Peter	Paul		
Dr. Mary	Janning		
Dr. Joe	Rose		
Dr. Ella	Jackson		
Dr. Connie	Bush		
Dr. Sam	Smart		

QUESTIONS TO ASK

	Name	Phone #	OK
1. Who is your Doctor?			
2. Who is your Attorney?			
3. Who is your CPA?			
4. Who is your Boss?			
5. Who is your the most successful person you know?			
6. Whose wedding did you attend last year?			
7. Who is your partner in sports?			
8. Who did you see a movie with recently?			

③ *You can get referrals consistently.*

Work with property and casualty agents

Spend the next seven days talking with property and casualty agents. However, we should not repeat the old story, "Let me work your files, and we'll split the commissions." Propose a strategy that will work, that will make sense, and that you and the property and casualty agent will easily find agreeable.

What is that strategy? You give the property and casualty agent 50 names, addresses, and phone numbers from your client files. In turn, you will receive 50 names, addresses, and telephone numbers from the property and casualty agent's client files. Each of you should call these "new prospects" only after the prospects have received a note that says,

> Mr. Jones,
>
> In the next few days, you will receive a call from_____ with_____. I have asked him to call you personally because of the extra services that he is willing to provide to you at no extra charge.
>
> We are quite proud to be able to make these services available to our clients. Whenever we can help our clientele, we do so.
>
> Sincerely,

Why does this strategy work? It is reciprocal. Both of you get 50 prospects. If both of you win, you will have the opportunity to receive an additional 50 names. If it becomes one-sided, the agreement should end. Whenever you can work in a specialized area, you will gain more respect and be more successful. For example, you know how to help people accumulate more money for retirement and the agent knows how to protect their home and car. However, you should meet with several agents before selecting one. Solicit testimonials. Remember, this strategy works because your clients know that you would only introduce them to a professional you respect.

Join forces with a younger associate

If you have been in the business for many years, another excellent way for you to meet referrals is through a younger associate. In essence, that associate "bird-dogs" for you. You win because you meet more people. The younger associate wins because he or she sells the services of you, the seasoned professional. The younger associate also wins by having the opportunity to become a seasoned professional faster because of the time spent with you. What's even more important, the clients win because they get the enthusiasm of a younger associate and the depth of a professional.

The key to getting referrals

During some of our training seminars, I will look around the room and ask one of the attendees for a five-dollar bill. I will hold the five-dollar bill in my right hand. Then I will ask another attendee, "May I please see your watch?" I will hold that watch in my left hand. I then ask one of the attendees to come up and stand by me in the front of the room. When that attendee comes to the front of the room, I say to the seminar audience,

> A few moments ago, I didn't have this five-dollar bill. I didn't have this watch, and I didn't have this associate to my left. But now I do. Why? Because I asked.

You, too, should ask. You should ask for the appointment . . . for the order . . . and for referrals.

Proven referral-creating scripts

Number 1

A great time to ask for a referral would be at the close.

I am going to assume that you want to get started. I only need three things.

The first thing: answers to a few questions on this application.

The second thing: a check to get started.

And the last thing I need are the first names of ten neighbors so I can help them in the same way that I helped you. Which of these neighbors (pointing to the names in your Referral Folder) do you know on a first-name basis?

(Continued on next page)

3 *You can get referrals consistently.*

(Proven referral-creating scripts continued)

However, after getting the first name, go directly to the application. You will return to the Referral Folder after the application is completed and you have the check. There is only one thing better than referrals . . . a completed application.

Number 2

Another great time to ask for referrals is at an annual review and after you have reviewed all of the benefits of owning the policy.

> When we first met I mentioned that I received compensation in two different ways: from my company and from you in the way of referrals if you thought I had helped you. Have I helped you? (Pause for response)

> Which of these neighbors (Point to your Referral Folder) do you know on a first-name basis?

Number 3

Another time to ask for referrals is during a service call. Whether you are addressing portfolio rebalancing, asset allocation, change of beneficiary, withdrawals, surrenders, exchanges, or delivering a death benefit, you now have another opportunity to ask for referrals.

> Are you satisfied with the services that I have provided to you? (Pause for response) The reason that I ask you that question is that every business person wants his business to grow. And the easiest way for my business to grow is if you could allow me to help some of your neighbors, associates, and friends as I have helped you. Which of these neighbors (pointing to your Referral Folder) do you know on a first-name basis?

Number 4

Another way to acquire referrals is to schedule referral meetings. The sole purpose of these meetings is to meet with your existing clients. We recommend that the meeting be kept short, concise, and to the point. And remember that you have only one objective during that meeting—to collect referrals.

Telephone Script for Referral Appointment

"When we first met, I explained to you that I get compensated in two ways. And, one of those ways was from you in the way of referrals. Now I don't expect you to know who wants any of my services. I just want to show you some names of people I would like to contact. It would only take 15 minutes of your time, and you can tell me if you know any of these people on a first-name basis. When would be a more convenient time to get together for 15 minutes? Is Monday good, or is Tuesday better?"

We have already discussed how to get referrals and when to ask for referrals. However, all of the above is meaningless if you just stockpile these names and never call them. A key component to our Referral Strategy is to contact every qualified referral no longer than seven days after you obtained permission from your clients to use their names.

Why within seven days? The key to this entire book is doing today what can be done tomorrow. The key to selling success is trying to avoid deep valleys in production, deep valleys and inconsistencies caused by not having a routine system.

Therefore, you should call every qualified referral. What should you say? First, you should read our chapter on how to use the phone successfully. Second, you should use any of the following phone scripts.

3 *You can get referrals consistently.*

Referral phone scripts

Mr. Smith, this is Bill Harris. Steve Jones is a client of mine. I hope that this is a good time to talk. I may be able to help you (see #1 below) just as I have with Steve. By the way, I hear that (see #2 below); info you may have entered in the "Special Interests section of your Referral Folder.

The reason for my call is to find the most convenient time for both of us to get together next week for 15 minutes. (Brief pause) Is Tuesday good, or is Thursday better?

1. a. defer current taxes on your investment earnings
   b. diversify properly
   c. protect the people you love
   d. reduce risk and increase your returns

2. By the way, I hear that you . . .

   a. are a basketball fan. Who is your favorite team?
   b. play tennis. Where do you play?
   c. golf. What is your handicap?
   d. enjoy the theater. Which plays have you seen recently?

Overcoming objections during phone calls to referrals

Not every referral conversation goes well. In fact, there can be only two things that can occur during a referral conversation. The conversation can go well or the conversation does not go well because you hear an objection.

If the conversation goes well, you book an appointment. If the conversation does not go well, you overcome the phone objection by using any one of our proven phone techniques. However, if another objection is raised, it is often best to thank referrals for their time, ask permission if you can call again and move on to your next referral. Why ask permission to call back? As you'll read in our phone section, your success rate during the second phone call will be much higher. Why? The referral has already spoken to you. The person will have already received one or more of your notes or letters from you. The referral will have already spoken to your client.

How to deal with the protective administrative assistant

When contacting referrals at work, you may encounter a "sergeant" who is specifically trained to prevent sales professionals like ourselves from talking to the boss. In the Phone section of this manual, we have provided proven techniques in order to deal with a "sergeant." However, when in a referral scenario, it is necessary to make minor adjustments in your dialogue. For example,

You: This is Bill Harris. Brian, please.

Sergeant: The reason you are calling?

You: Brian's friend, Steve Jones, is one of my clients. (smile in voice) Please tell Brian that Bill Harris is on the line, (no pause, but smile) thank you.

Sergeant: What is this regarding?

You: About income taxes. It will only take a few moments, (no pause, but smile) thank you.

The key ingredients of the above dialogue are obvious. You are confident. You are polite and warm, but at the same time, you are also firm. You will notice that by immediately saying "thank you" at the end of your every response you are not asking a question. You are making a statement. When the "sergeant" asked for the reason that you were calling, there would be nothing wrong if you asked the sergeant for his or her name. Then you could use the name after thank you.

An organized plan

Organization is the key to success. You must have written goals. You must have a plan. The major reason for mediocre years is poor prospecting and poor referral-creating approaches. The reason for poor skills is the lack of a system, a plan, and an organized way to acquire results.

(Continued on next page)

3 *You can get referrals consistently.*

(An organized plan continued)

A plan will help us become more organized because we will be using a proven system that removes all inconsistencies of low and high production weeks. A system will reduce and eliminate the anxiety that we often encounter when we do not have enough commissions coming in over the next four weeks. Anxiety occurs as a result of the lack of a system.

How do you begin getting referrals? Remember, preparing to get referrals is a mental process which begins with having the right attitude. And you will begin to get referrals when you consistently use our Referral Folder and Referral System by doing Referral Preparation in advance and asking the right questions.

Additional referral strategies

Network with other professionals such as CPAs and or attorneys. How do you begin networking? First, you should acquire their names. After you have acquired these names, send brochures to 20 of them per week. Call each and every one of those 20 individuals and introduce yourself.

> Hello, Mr. Jones, my name is_____and I am with_____. The purpose of my call is that I would like to meet with you, introduce my services, and the types of clients I have. I specialize in the_____market and many of my clients, from time to time, have a need for tax advice (or counsel). Needless to say, I am looking for a CPA (or attorney) to whom I can refer my customers. I am also looking for professionals such as yourself who are willing to refer their clients to me. However, that can only be done after I have earned your respect and trust. I was wondering if there might be a convenient time for the two of us to get together. Would Monday be good, or would Tuesday be better?

The purpose of having appointments with professionals is for us to have the opportunity to introduce ourselves and our company, to discuss the services we provide, and to establish rapport. The professionals we meet can, in turn, do the same.

6 Referral sources

Let's summarize in general and address the ideal sources for referrals. In fact, referral sources can be broken down into six groups:

1. All of your clients.
2. All vendors that you do business with on a regular basis.
3. All of your acquaintances.
4. Centers of influence. Your doctor, CPA, attorney.
5. Prospects who would have said "yes" to you if they had had the money or the need.
6. Corporate clients.

Should we pay for referrals?

Occasionally, people will ask me if gifts should be given to people who give us referrals. My feeling is a strong NO!

We recall one of our sales representatives saying to us that a person was willing to give us a referral if we gave him one of our books for free. My response was "no" People should refer a friend or associate to us only if they respect us and our products.

When your clients respect you, they will help.

3 *You can get referrals consistently.*

How to get referrals from clients who are reluctant to give you referrals

We have discussed how to deal with the objections we are certain to hear from referrals. That is the real world. But the real world will also give us situations when our clients do not want to give us referrals. When soliciting referrals from a client, and when we suspect reluctance, we should use the following words:

> "If one of your friends walked in right now, would you introduce him to me? (Pause for response) Of course you would. And that's all I am asking from you today. Can you give me the first names of some of your neighbors? What are Mr. & Mrs. Phillips first names?"

How to get written testimonials from clients and prospects

One important strategy for obtaining more referrals is to get our prospects and clients to verbalize how they feel about the services we have provided for them.

Dr. Jones, what have you appreciated the most about how I conduct my business? (Short pause, but if no response add) How I have shown you how to diversify your retirement money? Or that we were able to defer current taxes on your bank earnings?

After you get a positive response say,

> If we put what you just said on paper, I could show it to other doctors who also have a group practice. You wouldn't mind, would you?

Needless to say, use letters from clients whenever possible. In fact, use the letter below. All you need to do is obtain your clients' signatures.

> Dear Colleagues,
>
> Bill Harris helped us a great deal with our retirement plans. I recommend you spend time with Bill. He will probably be able to help you like he did with us.
>
> Thank you,
> Dr. Peter F. Schmitt

3

You can get referrals consistently.

In dollars and cents, what are the financial rewards associated with getting referrals consistently?

Question_____Assumed Answer

- How many sales did you make last month? _____ 4
- How many clients did you see last month? _____ 16
- Add lines 1 and 2. _____ 20
- Multiple the number on line 3 by 10_____ 200

(10 should be the minimum number of referrals received at each appointment)

- Pessimistically, assume that only 5% of these referrals will be new clients. _____ 10
- Multiply an average commission of $2,000 times $20,000 the number of new clients. (10)

If you had used our Referral Folder and the other proven strategies in this secret, you would have had a minimum of 200 referrals, 10 new clients, and $20,000 in commissions. Do you have 200 referrals to contact this month?   Probably not, but you will next month when you use a smarter, more reliable, more intelligent, more practical way to get referrals.

In closing, reflect on all of the things you can do to help more referrals. Educate clients on how they pay you (in referrals) if they are satisfied. Spend more time on Referral Preparation by gathering the names of people you want as clients. Use our Referral Folder strategy and our proven approaches using the right words. Call referrals on the phone using the right phone skills and scripts. Use centers of influence and the ideal sources for referrals. Above all, care about your clients and their families. When you do, referrals will come so much easier.

Summary: In this secret, you learned

- how to build a referral-creating attitude

- referral-creating approaches

- how to use the Referral Folder

- how to work with a property and casualty agent

- why to work with a younger associate

- proven referral phone scripts

- how to overcome objections during phone calls to referrals

- how to deal with the protective administrative assistant

- additional referral strategies

- six different referral sources

- whether we should pay for referrals

- how to get referrals from reluctant clients

- how to get written testimonials from clients and prospects

- the financial rewards of getting referrals

3 *You can get referrals consistently.*

---

1. Which section of the Referral Folder are you most interested using?

   Please circle your choice.

   • Neighbors
   • At Work
   • Professional
   • Probing Questions

2. Circle correct answer.

   a) A sale with a referral is a career.
   b) A sale without a referral is short term success.
   c) Both

3. Which two ways are you paid?

   1. _____

   2. _____

4. Which question will you no longer have to ask?

   a) Who do you know that might be interested in an annuity?

   b) Who do you know that might be interested in life insurance?

   c) Who do you know that might be interested in health insurance?

   d) All of the above.

Answers: 2, c, 3. 1-Commision, 2- Referral, 4. d

secret **4**

You can overcome almost every objection at the point of sale.

O ne of the easiest ways to achieve a higher level of success is to learn proven, easy-to-follow strategies to overcoming any objection. Objections, expressed or implied, general or specific, genuine or artificial, arise at the point of sale. A successful insurance and investment professional must learn how to anticipate each of these types of objections in advance and must learn how to overcome them easily.

Last year, objections may have been the one major barrier that prevented you from achieving selling success. This year, you will handle every objection using a proven selling strategy and time-tested scripts.

4 *You can overcome almost every objection at the point of sale.*

You will learn in this secret how to get objections surfaced and how to isolate, address, and overcome those objections. We provide two simple scripts that work for almost every objection and the best responses to different objections. This section can mean thousands of dollars in extra commissions for you. More importantly, this section can affect how many people you help.

Objections that prospects have been using for 30 years

Shouldn't we begin anticipating these objections in advance and learning the best ways to overcome them? This secret teaches you how to overcome each of these objections easily.

"Now is not the best time."

"Contact me later."

"I have a friend in the business."

"I can do better with my money."

"I would like to discuss it with my spouse."

"I never tie up my money for longer than a year."

"I would like to think about it."

"Let me read the brochure first."

"Is it insured like the FDIC?"

"I would like to talk to my CPA about it."

"I don't like annuities."

"I have no money."

The 4 important steps toward overcoming any objection

The most effective way to deal with objections successfully is to learn these four steps.

1. Learn how to uncover the objection.

2. Learn how to isolate the objection you have just uncovered.

3. Learn how to address the objection you have just uncovered and isolated.

4. Learn how to close after you have uncovered, isolated, and addressed the objection.

We risk $1,250 in commissions in every sales interview. That is approximately how much we risk in commissions by not knowing the best sales presentation, the best ways to uncover needs, and the best ways to discover solutions to the needs of our prospects. Twelve hundred and fifty dollars is too much to risk by simply not knowing how to overcome the objections that we know we will hear, since these are the same objections that prospects have been saying for 30 years. Isn't it about time we learn how easy it is to overcome almost any objection?

You can overcome almost every objection at the point of sale.

4

How to uncover the objection

Our first responsibility is to uncover our prospect's real objection. Many prospects and clients give brush-off responses without giving their real objections such as "Sounds great." "Let me think about it." These are nice, diplomatic, polite ways to curtail the decision-making process. We use them ourselves in our business and personal lives to avoid confrontations. Please reflect on the last time you had a disappointing meal. What did you say when the waitress brought the check and asked you how everything was? You probably smiled and said, "It was very nice." We do to others the same thing that prospects do to us. We all create these pleasant-sounding words that do not represent how we truly feel.

> "Sounds great, let me think about it."
>
> "Cool, let me discuss it with my spouse."
>
> "Very interesting! I'll review this with my accountant."

Prospects give us brush-off responses for four reasons. One reason is that they are unaware that they have a need or they do not see the benefit to solving that need now. The second reason we hear brush-off responses is because the prospect prefers not to debate or discuss the real objection. The third reason we hear brush-off responses is because anxiety appears with saying yes. The fourth reason is that you have not yet created a bond of rapport and trust. As a sales professional, you must learn how to address brush-off responses effectively.

Here are a few examples of some brush-off responses:

> "I would like to think about it."
>
> "Sounds great."
>
> "Let me read over the brochure first."
>
> "Let me talk it over with my spouse."

One way to get the objection out in the open is to use one easy-to-remember word: specifically

Prospect's objection
I would like to think about it.

Your response
What specifically would you like to think about?

Prospect's objection
Let me read the brochure first.

Your response
What specifically would you like to read about?

If there is a response and the prospect tells you what she wants to specifically think about, you have successfully uncovered her objection. This approach will allow you to bring your prospect to closure, or you will uncover your prospect's objection. Either way, you win.

Are there other words that can help you get the objection out in the open? Yes, they are why and when.

Prospect's objection
Now is not the best time.

Your response
"Why isn't now the best time? (Friends, you are not being pushy. It could be a genuine objection like a wedding or an important business reason.)

Prospect's objection
I'm still undecided. Contact me later!

Your response
"When would you like me to call you later? Tomorrow? (if no quick response) Next week?

④ *You can overcome almost every objection at the point of sale.*

How to isolate that objection

However, we must know how to isolate the objection after the objection has been uncovered if we really want our sales career to skyrocket.

The strategies that follow are ideal for isolating objections. Please note that regardless of what the prospects say, you often respond with the same thing. If they echo another objection after you ask the question, always address the most recent objection.

Prospect's objection
I would like to discuss it with my spouse. (or CPA)

Your response
"Let's assume that your spouse (or CPA) were to OK this. Do you know of any other reason why you would not go ahead with this plan?"

Prospect's objection
Now is not the right time

Your response
"Sir, if this were the right time, do you know of any other reason why you would not go ahead with this plan?"

Prospect's objection
I do not have money.

Your response
"If you did have the money, do you know of any other reason for you not to go ahead with this plan?"

Prospect's objection
I never make decisions the first time I hear about something."

Your response
"Sir, if this were not the first time, do you know of any other reason why you would not go ahead with this plan?"

2 ways to address the objection with accurate information

We now know how to get the objection uncovered and isolated. Now, let's learn how to address and overcome objections successfully by giving them an accurate layer of information.

#1 The "reason not to buy is the precise reason that they should buy"

Let's now paint a picture. You have uncovered your prospect's objection. You have isolated your prospect's objection by using the techniques on the previous pages. Use the following responses to address their objections. Please notice that the key to getting the objection addressed successfully is the important information you offer.

Prospect's objection
I have a friend in the business.

Your response
"That is the precise reason why you should be my client. You do not want your friend to know about your or your spouse's medical history, weight, etc. I want to be your advisor on important–and sometimes confidential–matters regarding your health and your money. Occasionally, these are matters that only you and your advisors should know about and perhaps not your friend. If I may, I would like to show you one additional benefit. May I?"

Prospect's objection
Now is not the best time.

Your response
"I can appreciate how you feel but this is the best time because the difference between starting now and starting later amounts to tens of thousands of dollars. May I show you what I mean?" *(Continued on next page)*

4

You can overcome almost every objection at the point of sale.

(#1 reason not to buy is the precise reason that they should buy continued)

Prospect's objection
I can get a higher return elsewhere.

Your response
"You probably can get a higher return elsewhere in some years but with that comes market risk and uncertainty. But since none of us have a crystal ball and future gains and losses with the stock market are uncertain, may I show you how an annuity gives you a guaranteed minimum return every year."

#2 The "feel/felt/found" approach but again offering new information

Prospect's objection
I would like to discuss it with my spouse.

Your response
I can appreciate how you feel. Many of my clients felt the same way. However they found that their spouse respected the decisions they made when it was about protecting the family. If I may, I would like to show you one additional benefit. May I?"

Prospect's Objection

We cannot afford it.

Your Response

"I can appreciate how you feel. Many of my clients initially felt the same way but they found that they could afford it if they simply got some of the money they spent on_____ (coffee, soda, or lunch) everyday and redirected it toward a premium that would provide a lot more value than_____ (a cup of coffee, a GIANT Coke, or a triple pounder with cheese)."

"May I now show you how an insurance premium of $195.00 a month can give you and your spouse more value than a large coffee every day?"

After showing them where to find the money, ask, "Do you now see that you can afford it? "(pause for a response) After they say yes to that question, "Earlier, you said that was the only thing holding you back. I assume that you want your wife, Kathleen, to be the primary beneficiary. What is your Social Security number?"

Prospect's Objection

I cannot afford it.

Your Response

"I can appreciate how you feel. Many of my clients initially felt the same way but they found that they could afford the extra insurance they needed if they _____
(changed how they paid the premiums on their current policies for the next year) or (if they changed the type of insurance they owned.)"

"May I show you how you can do that?"

After showing them where to find the money, ask, "Do you now see that you can afford it?"(pause for a response)

After they say yes to that question, "Earlier, you said that was the only thing holding you back. I assume that you want your wife, Kathleen, to be the primary beneficiary. What is your Social Security number?"

Prospect's Objection

Why should I buy a permanent life product when I can buy term and invest the difference?

Pick 1 of the following 4 responses

1) "I can appreciate how you feel. Many of my clients initially felt the same way but they found that term insurance disappears when they are most apt to need it. May I show you some statistical data in a new book titled *75 Secrets* that I just bought that discusses longer life expectancy?"

2) "I can appreciate how you feel. Many of my clients initially felt the same way but they found that the premium for term insurance becomes almost unaffordable when you are most apt to need life insurance. May I show you what the term premium is for a 60 year old?"

3) "I can appreciate how you feel. Many of my clients initially felt the same way but they found that they did NOT save or invest the difference. May I show you new statistical data from a new book *75 Secrets* I just bought that shows how difficult it is for people to save?" *(Continued on next page)*

4

You can overcome almost every objection at the point of sale.

(Buy term and invest the difference continued)

4) "I can appreciate how you feel. Many of my clients initially felt the same way but they found that they lost 40% of their money when they invested the difference in 2008 and in 2009. May I show you how to get the best of both worlds, affordable premiums and guaranteed values?"

After showing them, ask, " Do you now see that term life insurance is not always the least expensive way? (pause for a response)

After they say yes to that question, "Earlier, you said that was the only thing holding you back. I assume that you want your wife, Kathleen, to be the primary beneficiary. What is your Social Security number?

Prospect's Objection
I have life insurance at work.

Your Response
"I can appreciate how you feel. Many of my clients initially felt the same way but they found that they had NO insurance after ------------------------(they left that job) or (they were laid off) or (they were fired) or (the company closed their doors) or (the company decreased their benefits in order to save money) May I show the best way to get individual insurance so it can not be taken away from you?"

FYI Naturally, the best time is when they are still insurable. And, they will never be younger than they are now.

Prospect's Objection
I need to do some research on the company before I make a any decision.

Your Response

"I can appreciate how you feel. Many of my clients initially felt the same way but they found that the only research available was the same research that I found. May I show it to you? It it is in my car."

Prospect's Objection

I already own enough insurance or I do not need life insurance.

Your Response

"If I can show you an interesting way to calculate how much life insurance is enough, one of 3 things will occur.

You will find out that you have enough life insurance. Or, you will find out that you have too much or not enough. You win in any event. May I show you?"

Summary: Part 1 of 2

And after showing the prospect important information that convinces them otherwise, ask:

Do you see that now is the best time?

Do you see now that you can afford it?

Do you see now that term is not always the least expensive way?

Do you see now that life insurance at work is very temporary?

Do you see now that you have all the research you need?

Do you see now that you do not have enough life insurance?

After they say yes to that question, "Earlier, you said that was the only thing holding you back? I assume that you want your wife, Kathleen, to be the primary beneficiary? What is your Social Security number?"

Summary: Part 2 of 2

You need only two approaches to address most objections.

#1 The reason not to buy is the precise reason to buy. With that approach, you offer new information for them to consider.

#2 Using the words feel, felt, found and again offering new information.

You can overcome almost every objection at the point of sale.

However, there are unique objections when those two approaches will not work. Let's discuss those objections now since they deserve unique responses in order for them to be overcome consistently.

Prospect's Objection

I don't like the surrender charges.

Your response

"If you were to purchase 1,000 shares of stock valued at $20 per share, what would you be able to sell the stock for two years from now? You don't know, do you?

If you were to invest $100,000 in muni-bonds, what would you be able to sell those muni-bonds for two years from now if interest rates increase appreciably? You don't know, do you?

If you were to purchase that gorgeous $900,000 home overlooking the fifth fairway, what would you be able to sell it for two years from now? Plus, how long would it take you to sell it? You don't know, do you?" *(Continued on next page)*

(I don't like surrender charges continued)

In Secret 9, we discuss a wide variety of ways to discuss surrender charges.

The surrender charges are the second best thing about many of the products that we offer because they are expressed in the contract. In 99 percent of everything our prospects and clients buy, they have no idea what the selling price is going to be. However, they always know our selling price because it is specified in every non-MVA fixed annuity policy and non-variable life policy that we offer. Be proud of the surrender charge period. We can give people what they want–certainty, a guarantee, no surprises–a selling price for every year of their life.

When you really think about it, doesn't an actuary provide a surrender charge period to protect an insurance company from excess withdrawals and premature surrenders–in other words, a run on the bank?

Ask, "Would you rather have your money with an insurance company that is trying to protect itself from a run on the bank, or with an insurance company that is not trying to protect itself from a "run on the bank?"

In the past, some of us went searching for insurance companies that were losing money. That's right. We went looking for insurance companies with the highest interest rates, the shortest surrender charge periods, the highest commissions, and the most liquidity. Some of us went searching for insurance companies that were losing money and some of us found them.

These days, insurance and investment professionals are beginning to look for profitable insurance companies to stand behind their clients' desires, needs, objectives, and savings dollars. There must be three winners. The insurance company must win…we must win, but above all, our clients must win. Whenever we think we need just two winners, there can be three losers.

---

*We are not saying that an insurance company with lower penalties is weaker than an insurance company with higher penalties.

4 *You can overcome almost every objection at the point of sale.*

I never tie my money up for longer than a year

Often, when selling a financial product with surrender charges, customers will say that they never tie their money up for longer than a year. When you hear this objection, use this proven dialogue:

You: "How long have you been rolling over your money at the bank from one year to the next?"

Prospect: "10 years."

You: "There are 365 days in one year. How many days are there in 10 years?" (Pause and allow your customer to answer.)

Prospect: "3,650 days."

You: "If I understand you correctly, you have been renewing your money at the bank from one year to the next for the last 3,650 days. Am I correct?"

Prospect: "Yes."

You: "At the end of each of the last 10 years, you have had a grace period at the bank where you have had penalty-free access to your principal and interest. You could do anything you wished with these dollars without premature loss of interest penalties. How many days were in that grace period?"

Prospect: "Seven days."

You: "And, you have had 7 days at the end of each year and you have been doing this for 10 years. Seven days times 10 equals…"

Prospect: "70 days."

Your prospects will begin to realize the slight chance of their emergency arising during these 70 special days. That's right. During the last 3,650 days, they had only 70 magical days of penalty-free access to their bank principal and interest.

You: "As I stated earlier, our penalties do not reappear every year. In fact, they disappear in seven short years.** Which means in years 8, 9, 10, and thereafter, there will be no penalties at all on this product. Which product in your opinion has more penalty-free liquidity: an account with 70 penalty-free total liquidity days or this product with 1,095 penalty-free total liquidity days?" (365 times 3, in other words, years 8, 9, and 10.)"

** *Assumes a surrender charge period of 7 years.*

The safety objection

Unquestionably, safety is on the minds of our prospects and clients. The media is beginning to talk about the same insurance companies that our Moms and Dads discussed in the dens of our homes. We can no longer use the exclusive strategy that we used to use…

> "My company is rated _____ by _____."
> In other words, one rating from one of the fine rating services.

When prospects hear that, they respond, "Sure, and so was _____ Life Insurance Company and so was _____ Life Insurance Company."

Am I saying that rating services are not important? No! In fact, I feel just the opposite. Rating services are important. However, we may need to say more than just one rating from one service. What else do we need? If you look at the life insurance companies that did have problems over the past years, some of them had two things in common. One thing that many insurance companies had in common was where they had been investing. Therefore, one way to distinguish yourself from some of the companies that have had problems is to say:

> "Not all insurance companies are created equal. Allow me to tell you where my insurance company has its money."

Therefore, one way to convey safety is to discuss the insurance company that stands behind the guarantees. And, where your company has its money allows you to distinguish your company from the companies that experienced problems since guarantees are as strong as the insurance company making the guarantees.

4 *You can overcome almost every objection at the point of sale.*

Are the dollars insured like the FDIC insures bank deposits?

No matter how often you have explained that the guarantees are as strong as the insurance company making the guarantees, the prospect is still going to ask you,

> "Are my dollars insured like the FDIC insures bank deposits?"

After you hear your prospect ask that question, your conversation should be similar to the following script.

> You: "That is a very good question. No, it is not, but may I ask you a question?" (Pause for response) Do you own a home?

Prospect: "Yes."

> You: "If you were to sell your home today, what would you ask for it?"

Prospect: "$600,000."

> You: "That's terrific, a $600,000 home. I have one last question. Do you have your home insured?"

Prospect: "Of course!"

> You: "You were wise to have selected an insurance company to insure and guarantee your single most valuable asset, your $600,000 home. You are again being wise since you are again selecting an insurance company to stand behind the dollars that you are placing in this annuity today. Doesn't it feel good that strong insurance companies can stand behind your home, your car, your life, your health, and your money?"

We select insurance companies to insure our single most valuable asset, our $100,000, $200,000, $300,000, or $600,000 homes, don't we? We select insurance companies to insure our cars and our jewelry. We select insurance companies to insure our ability to bring home a paycheck each week (disability income). We select insurance companies to insure our health, our retirement, and our lives. *(Continued on next page)*

(Are the dollars insured like the FDIC insures bank deposits continued)

In Secret 12, you'll learn how to focus on bank dollars.

We must get prospects to use their intellect. If they do, they will appreciate knowing that insurance companies are standing behind their home, their car, their health, their retirement, their lives, and everyone they love. When we get prospects to use their intellect, they will begin to appreciate how much peace of mind we have given them in the past, how much peace of mind we give them now, and how much peace of mind we can give them in their future.

NOTE: This approach should be preceded with the real bottom-line answer, "A guarantee is as strong as the insurance company making the guarantees."

The real skeleton in our closet

Previously, I mentioned that some of the insurance companies that recently experienced problems shared two things. Where they were investing was one of those things. The other thing that some of the insurance companies had in common was a run on the bank.

Few institutions–including insurance companies can survive 25,000 phone calls a week with billions and billions of dollars being surrendered in a short period of time. Fortunately, a run on the bank is something that we can often control and prevent. We must recognize that selling fear damages our careers. The small amount of money we can make on one, two, or three surrenders, replacements, and 1035 exchanges is dramatically less than the money we would have made if we had kept our industry strong.

Instead of saying, "Oh, you don't have that insurance company, do you?," let's learn how to find other dollars from a different industry. This is preferable to moving the same dollars from one insurance company to the next.

We must stop selling fear. We should start selling needs. We must stop selling the interest rate. We should start selling needs. We must stop selling price. We should start selling needs. We must ignite and fuel our own career success. And, career success means repeat business from clients and repeat referrals and a strong insurance industry.

4
You can overcome almost every objection at the point of sale.

Anticipate all objections

We as insurance and investment professionals must anticipate all objections. We must role-play and rehearse. When was the last time you rehearsed your sales presentation? Baseball's Hall of Fame Ted Williams practiced every day. Why don't you? Too many sales people try something out for the first time while they're with a prospect. That is not the time to wing it. The time to wing it is at home or at the office or in your car.

When you hear the objection at the point of sale, you must:

1. Listen attentively to the objection.

2. Show the prospect that you understand and respect the objection. "I can appreciate how you feel about (restate their objection)."

3. Address and overcome the objection by using reason and emotion.

4. Solicit acknowledgement from the prospect that the objection is no longer a concern.

5. Close.

The average sale involves 3 objections

A recent survey reported that an average sale involves three objections. Are you walking away too soon? Review the appointments you had last week. Visualize each appointment. Did you leave after the first objection? The second? The third? Once again, let's remember the most important priority, our prospect. Prospects must be sure that they are making decisions which are in their best interest. All we want to do is to assist them in making the wise decision. All we want to do is to remove the anxiety that everyone experiences when making a decision.

Talking it through

We'd all like to remain in the status quo. The status quo provides tranquility. Change creates anxiety. Overcoming objections is perceived by some people as being manipulative. However, nothing could be further from the truth. Overcoming objections gives prospects a new layer of information. Overcoming objections is "talking it through."

I recall when Mary and I were considering a move to California. We spent five days looking at one house after another. Not only were we going through a change of 3,000 miles, we were also going through the change between a California home and a Connecticut home. One home had a big backyard and no pool. The other home had a tiny backyard with a large pool. One home had a cedar-shake roof, the other had a red Spanish tile roof. And, one home was valued at just 33% of what the new home would cost.

Unquestionably, I experienced a high level of anxiety and tension when we found the home that Mary and the realtor decided was in our best interest. Did I want to say "yes" right away? No. Did I want to "talk it through?" Yes. That is exactly what we did with the realtor. We talked and we talked. There were objections. We examined them. Mary and the realtor both heard me say, "It costs too much. It's too large." But, every time we talked it through, I realized that the home was not too large and not too expensive. Mary and the realtor lessened my anxiety by "talking it through."

This is what you should be learning from this secret. You are learning to talk it through. *(Continued on next page)*

4

You can overcome almost every objection at the point of sale.

However, that realtor had something special. In fact, she had the same something special that I want from every professional with whom I do business. She had my trust and respect, and we had rapport. A professional with the greatest closing techniques, trained by the best sales trainer, will not succeed until respect and trust have been earned.

In the same way, there must be rapport, trust, and respect between you and the prospect. When was the last time you bought something from a salesperson that you did not like? If you have, didn't you think less of that product? Wasn't there a degree of uncertainty about whether you had done the right thing? And, how many referrals did you give that salesperson. That's right. None.

Acquiring product knowledge, caring about your prospect more than yourself, being a caring listener, being sincere, and all of the other traits addressed in this book will help you achieve a higher level of success. However, when you have all of the above plus you know how to get objections uncovered, isolated, addressed, and closed, then you are truly a professional who will have a dramatic effect on the emotional and financial lives of thousands of people.

What you have learned from this secret? You have learned to talk it through. You are not trying to get someone to do something that he or she does not want to do. You are only assisting the prospect to hurdle that moment of tension so they make a decision that is in their best interests.

Summary: In this secret, you learned

- the 4 important steps toward overcoming any objection

- how to uncover the objection

- how to isolate that objection

- how to address the objection

- the reason not to buy is the reason to buy

- the "feel/felt/found" approach

- the "Let me read the brochure first" objection

- the "I don't like the surrender charges" objection

- the "I never tie my money up for longer than a year" objection

- the "Safety" objection

- "are the dollars insured like FDIC?" objection

- about the real skeleton in our closet

- how to anticipate all objections

- how the average sale involves 3 objections

- the importance of talking it through

4 *You can overcome almost every objection at the point of sale.*

Overcoming Objection Quiz

1. The first step toward overcoming any objection is:

   a) uncover
   b) isolate
   c) address

2. The word that often gets the objection surfaced is:

   a) why
   b) specifically
   c) let's go ahead with it
   d) a & b

3. The best way to address a genuine objection is:

   a) to always say the same thing
   b) to smile
   c) to address it with accurate information

Answers: 1. a 2. d 3. c

secret **5**

You can have a lot of success with public speaking.

It is smart business whenever we can give 25 to 50 people the opportunity to say "yes" to us in one hour's time. In this secret, you'll be given tips that will make your seminars sales-creating. You will learn from the mistakes, the successes, and the experiences from more than 2,000 seminars. Sit back and relax. You're about to learn what few people know: how to use seminars to reduce prospecting worries.

5 *You can have a lot of success with public speaking.*

How to eliminate anxiety about speaking

Many people fear speaking in front of a group of people. In fact, more people fear public speaking than fear flying. I can understand this fear because prior to 1985, I had only given four seminars. Why? I was afraid of them.

Anxiety! How can we conquer it? There are four steps.

- One is knowing, not memorizing, our topic.

- The second step is to recall in our mind what we are really doing at the seminar. We are teaching people the importance of thinking about their money.

- The third step to lessen the anxiety. Simply imagine the worst possible thing happening like an attendee could ask you a question and you do not know the answer. If that were to happen, we would simply say:

> Sir, that's a good question. Rather than give you a partial answer, I would like to research it further, and get back to you. May I?

> or

> Sir, I do not know the answer to that question, but I do know someone who does. I'll get the answer for you first thing tomorrow morning.

We are now prepared for the worst. We can now stop worrying. The key to conquering anxiety is to remain calm and handle situations to the best of our ability.

- The fourth step toward lessening anxiety is realizing that the presentation you are giving is nothing more than a conversation between you and them.

22 speaking tips to follow

1. Be yourself

   If you are enthusiastic, fine. If you are quiet and firm, fine. The key is to use your own personality as a speaker, and don't "borrow" from anyone else.

2. Care about the audience

   Not too long ago, we considered having one of our seminars professionally filmed, using a five-person film crew. However, our first thought was the audience. We were concerned that the lights, cameras, and members of the film crew would distract the attendees and they would miss some of the information being presented. We decided against filming.

3. Place the needs of your seminar audience before your own. Make sure they are comfortable at all times. Remember to treat them the same way you would treat a guest in your home.

4. Maintain eye contact

   Always maintain eye contact with the attendees. This creates a more comfortable situation for both you and them.

5. Use humor sparingly (unless you are a comedian)

   We never begin a seminar with a joke. One of two things can happen when you do begin with a joke. The audience can either laugh or not laugh. And, when the attendees do not laugh, you know and they know that you wanted them to laugh. Do not begin a seminar with uncertainty. Begin a seminar with control and strength. For example, we spend countless hours writing and rearranging the words in the beginning 60 seconds for each seminar and web conference. We still rehearse those lines when getting ready for the event. *(Continued on next page)*

5

You can have a lot of success with public speaking.

(Use humor sparingly continued)

Not too long ago, I was doing the same seminar five days in a row in five different cities. I began each seminar by telling an amusing story about my son, Will. I told the story exactly the same way each time, using the same tone, the same diction, and the same delivery. In the first four cities, the attendees were rolling in the aisles laughing. But in San Diego, my story was greeted with complete silence.

The problem with telling a joke or story at the beginning of a seminar is there is a chance that the attendees will not find it amusing. Getting off to a good start is important. Start off with an idea they will find helpful and informative since that sets the stage for what your seminar is about, ideas. Use humor during your presentation, but only after you have established a rapport with the audience.

6. Be well groomed

Being well groomed is important for the seminar speaker. We used to do as many as five real small seminars in one day. Mrs. H., my wife, would often say to me, "Bill, have you ever considered how you look at the end of the day giving that fifth seminar?" One day I was giving a seminar, and it happened to be the fifth seminar of the day. I was giving my presentation in an elegant meeting room. One entire wall of this room was lined with mirrors. As I was giving my presentation, I casually looked to the left, and I froze! I almost did not recognize myself! Mary was right. People can look very, very tired at the end of the day.

Thirty minutes prior to every seminar, you should take a quick look in the mirror and make sure you look your best.

7. Work the room and walk the room

   If you walk around the seminar room, you will keep your audience more interested in the information you're presenting. It is too easy for a seminar attendee to become distracted or daydream as it is. If you stay anchored in the same place, it is even more difficult for the attendees to stay alert.

   Also, do not use a podium in the traditional way. Using a podium creates a barrier between you and your audience. If you come into a room with a podium already set up for you, gently move it at an angle so your laptop can rest on it but the audience can still get a full view of you.

8. Questions

   Speakers differ on the issue of responding to spontaneous questions from the audience. We feel strongly that questions should not be encouraged during your presentation for three reasons:

   - Questions make the seminar much longer than it should be.

   - Some questions can throw you off the track.

   - Sometimes the questions are not very good and may require a long, long answer. And, if you refuse to give an answer, it may appear as if you are skirting the issue.

   At the beginning of the seminar, we suggest that you ask the attendees to hold their questions until the question-and-answer period which will follow your seminar.

9. Prepare visual aids carefully

Arrive at the seminar room 60 to 90 minutes before you are scheduled to speak and check several important items. Check the audio and visual equipment and the lighting. Since you should use visuals from your computer (or easel), the lights in the room normally will need to be adjusted. Therefore, before attendees begin to arrive, the lights in the room should be adjusted so that the front of the room is dimly lit so that the visuals on the screen may be seen clearly. In instances where lights cannot be dimmed, the bulbs in the hotel ceiling can easily be taken out by a special tool which all hotels have. The rest of the seminar room must be well lit so that eye contact can be maintained with the attendees at all times. People retain information 22 times longer if they see and hear it rather than just hear it. However, visuals should not be substituted for speaking. Instead, visuals should be used to enhance and emphasize what you're saying and visuals should contain the information you want them to remember. And, of course, please do not turn your back to the audience and read the "visual". Said a different way, would you feel comfortable if the heart surgeon who was performing a 5-way bypass on you was reading from one of his manuals?

10. Roll with the mistakes

You will be very, very disappointed if you expect your seminar to go perfectly. That is not to say you should not try your best. You should always try your best. We are only saying that you should not allow a problem to ruin a seminar for you. Just learn from your mistakes and try not to repeat them during your next seminar.

11. Use pauses during your presentation

   An excellent way to hold the concentration of the audience is to pause at the right time. If you have attended one of our seminars, you'll recall us saying, "My insurance license is about this large." Immediately 200-600 heads look up as I pause and show the size of my license using my hands.

12. Modulate your voice

   Lower and raise your voice when you want the audience's attention.

13. Use hand gestures

   Use hand gestures above the shoulder when referring to a series of items such as "1, 2, or 3" or "the second best, third best, the fourth best." Use hand gestures at chest level when you are expressing an emphatic point.

14. Smile but only if you feel like it

   If you do smile, it must be genuine. When you "feel" like smiling, then smile. Be sincere. Be friendly. Be yourself.

15. Greet the audience

   When the attendees begin arriving, make it a point to be at the door, shake their hand, and talk with them. Will this increase sales for you? I don't know. But it is good to meet the people that you will soon be helping. Remember the seminar is not about you. The seminar is about the attendees in the room. Try to mingle in the front of the room 15 minutes before the seminar begins. This is a secret way of getting comfortable with standing in the front of the room before the seminar begins. This one technique will remove 85% of the butterflies from your stomach before your seminar begins.

5 *You can have a lot of success with public speaking.*

16. Seminar invitations

You should mail a seminar invitation approximately two to three weeks before the seminar unless you are using "bulk mail". Who do you invite? You invite your existing clients first. When you only invite new people, you have to make two sales. First, why they should buy from you, and second, why they should buy your product. With your existing clients, you have only one sale to make: why they should buy your product.

When your clients call to R.S.V.P., you should say:

> Mr. Jones, I have you confirmed for our seminar on Wednesday night at the library downtown. Let me ask you one last question: Would you like to bring a friend or family member or neighbor with you?

One of the easiest ways to attract new prospects is to arrange for your existing clients to bring friends, family members, or neighbors to a seminar. Please note that Client Appreciation events will be discussed in more detail in Secret 8.

I realize that you may not have a large clientele and you are going to have to invite new prospects. Who should you invite? You should rent names from a mailing list broker. Which names should you rent? You should rent the names of people who are most apt to buy your product and those who live within 20 miles of the seminar site and your office if appointments take place in your office.

17. Mail the seminar invitation to the right types of people.

3 different seminars on individual retirement accounts, mortgage acceleration, or annuities may mean three different mailing lists. Know who your market is.

18. Avoid the high-income (and low-income) areas.

    In general, avoid the high-income areas as it relates to seminar invitations. Why?

    - They are being over-solicited.

    - They already have CPAs, attorneys, and other advisors that can become an obstacle to you initially.

19. Mailing invitations is not enough.

    Call your existing clients and former clients. Call referrals. Call prospects that have seen your presentation. Call those who have attended past seminars. Call the people whom received your invitations. Most mailing list brokers will provide you with the phone numbers (for a premium, in most instances). Pay it. It can be worth it! However, make sure that the name is not on the Do Not Call list. And, consider a person age 55 or older calling.

    When we use to speak in Southern California, as many as 600 brokers attended. Do you know why so many attended? Because we invited 10,000 agents to attend. We are in a numbers game, and you are in the same numbers game. You must mail and you must call.

20. Promote your seminar whenever possible.

    Consider all vendors with whom you do a great deal of business. Ask if they will leave your seminar invitation on their counters. Also, promote your seminars at all group functions. In addition, send a press release to each local newspaper.

20. Use your seminar invitation also as a stuffer.

    By preparing for your seminar event six to eight weeks in advance, it also allows you to use your seminar invitation as a stuffer and send it to people who get your newsletter, invoices, etc.

21. Join together with other agents.

    Ask other agents to invite their existing clients. You provide the speaking expertise. You provide the meeting room. You provide the audio and visual equipment. Any business that results from the seminar will be on a shared basis.

How to write the seminar invitation

1. The seminar title must grab the reader's attention.

2. The date and the location of the seminar must be easily readable.

3. The seminar invitation must impress. It must show substance. It must specifically state everything the invitees will learn at your seminar.

4. The outside of the seminar invitation must look too important to be thrown away. Consider trying an envelope that looks like a wedding invitation.

5. The seminar invitation must be packed with benefit-oriented copy plus the word FREE!, at least 2 times.

6. The seminar invitation should include a photograph of you, the speaker. Also, include your accomplishments in a brief and concise format.

7. The seminar invitation must conform to any rules and regulations set forth by your state department of insurance and/or broker/dealer and/or insurer.

4 things to do 6 to 8 weeks before your seminar

Pre-seminar preparation

1. Begin planning six to eight weeks before the seminar.

2. Pick a convenient and well-known site for your seminar. We recommend public libraries, museums, a bank's community room, a university, a restaurant, or even a movie theatre for a morning seminar. I like these types of sites because some of these are available for a modest charge (or free) and they also lend an aura of education, security, or uniqueness to your seminar.

   If you do a seminar at a hotel, you are often "thrown into a mixed bag" with other seminar vendors. However, if you are going to have a large seminar, you must use a hotel because hotels have the facilities to handle large groups of people.

3. Send out press releases.
   Create a short, concise press release using benefit-oriented copy. It should include what those who attend will learn, and it should be self-promotional. If possible, write a two to four-page booklet or article. Then you can begin to call yourself an author. There is little difference in the eyes of many people between an author of a four-page booklet and the author of a 350-page manual. Send the press release two weeks before the seminar to every newspaper in town and then again one week before the seminar. *(Continued on next page)*

5 *You can have a lot of success with public speaking.*

(4 things to do before your seminar continued)

4. Be focused on your seminar topic.

The topic you select should be one that people want to learn more about. One of the most important things about your seminar is the title. Review newspapers, though we do not recommend you advertise your seminar in newspapers other than issuing press releases. Observe community rooms and talk to librarians about recent seminars. Get a general idea of the titles of successful seminars. Then create a catchy, creative, and unique title. The number of people you invite, the number of people you call, and a catchy title on your seminar invitation are three things that will help you have a successful seminar.

What to do 90 minutes before the seminar

Remember to arrive at least 60 to 90 minutes before the attendees are scheduled to arrive. Check the lights, the audio and visual equipment, the set-up of the tables and chairs, the registration desk, and make sure that everything is running smoothly.

We recommend using classroom-style seating. In other words, set tables in front of the chairs. This classroom-style setup reminds the attendees that this is an educational seminar and encourages them to take notes. Leave a little pad of paper and a pen on each table for attendees. Nothing else. No other literature for them to review. Just a little pad so they can take notes.

Refreshments

If you would like to provide refreshments at your seminar, I recommend coffee, tea, soda, and cookies. But not cookies from a pastry shop. Cookies from your home. However, get permission from the hotel or restaurant first. And, the best time to get this permission is before you sign the paperwork. Be frugal when it comes to refreshments, especially when you are doing seminars at hotels. One cheese pastry can cost you $2.50 and one little glass of orange juice can be as much as $4.00. Some of our seminar hosts have paid well over $2,000 for coffee alone at our 400-plus seminars.

When the attendees arrive, greet everyone. Mill around, walk the room, work it, shake hands. Be polite. Be professional.

3 Things You Must Do In Order To Have A Successful Seminar

The biggest mistake that insurance and investment professionals make regarding seminars is they think they need a powerful seminar presentation with 30-50 visuals in order to succeed. Surprisingly, in order to succeed, you only need to accomplish 3 things.

1. You need to build rapport and trust with the audience. As they're listening to you, you want them to think or say to their spouse, "My, isn't he a nice man?"

2. You don't need to give the audience 30-50 different ideas; you only need to give them two or three ideas but they have to be unforgettable ideas such as our idea that shows the roller coaster ride of Bank CD interest rates over the past 50 years or what former Presidents of the United States said about the Economy or Social Security. Both of these films plus 6 more unforgettable ideas can be seen on our website www.75secrets.com in the DVD-ROM video section of the website. However, you do not have to use our unforgettable ideas, use yours such as the Rule Of 72 any of your other "A" material.

3. At every seminar, either you convince the audience that they need you or they convince you that you are not needed.

   With some degree of exaggeration, you could spend 90 % of the time talking about your favorite sports team and still have a successful seminar if they say to themselves or to their spouse:

   1. "Isn't he nice?"

   2. "Dear, wasn't that interesting when Mr. H. showed us the unbelievable volatility of having most of our money in the bank."

   3. "We really should get together with him. We need him."

   We need to accomplish the same 3 things at the point of sale.

5 *You can have a lot of success with public speaking.*

The ingredients to an ideal client seminar

1. Excite.

   You must motivate and excite. Show the attendees all of the benefits of your product and of doing business with you.

2. Educate mildly.

   You are not trying to educate the audience on how to become insurance agents, financial planners, or stockbrokers. Education should be done at the point-of-sale. The emphasis should be on excitement and benefits, not education.

3. Do not pass out any material before your seminar begins.

   There should be handouts, but they should only be available at the end of your presentation. If there are handouts, your attendees will be reading them while you're talking. When you are speaking, you do not want anything to distract you (or them) from your presentation.

4. Limit yourself to 45 minutes.

   Be brief! Your seminar presentation should only be 45 minutes long. If you are still talking after 60 minutes, you are losing money. You are there to inform and excite. You are not there to teach them everything about your product. Again, be brief.

5. You want to be graphic and visual.

   Use a computer, or pre-written easels. A computer is preferable. Remember that people retain information 22 times longer if they see it and hear it. The information that you show should be the information you want them to remember. Get prospects involved in what you are discussing by stimulating their senses.

6. End with a special questionnaire.

In Secret 10, we give you our seminar questionnaire.

We call the questionnaire special only because it works. At the end of your 45 minute seminar, pass out this questionnaire. The first two questions on the questionnaire are important. The first is, "Did you find this seminar informative?" Everyone is going to say "Yes." The second question is, "Would you like to be invited to more seminars?" Again, everyone is going to say "Yes." You are doing something very important here. You are getting the attendees into the routine of completing this form.

The next section of the questionnaire lists the needs that your products can solve. For example, reducing taxes on Social Security, more money later, probate, tax-advantaged income, inflation, estate taxes, etc. How you use the questionnaire at your seminar will determine the amount of business you will eventually write. Simply put, you do a quick commercial on how you can solve each particular need. Here is an example of what you can say at the seminar:

> "Many of you are upset about paying taxes on your Social Security income. I don't blame you. I have a special form here." Hold it up, then put it down. "It takes only three minutes to complete. Many of you are paying taxes unnecessarily. If you wish to reduce or eliminate those taxes, please make a check mark next to Social Security on this questionnaire."

Did I teach anyone in the audience how I solve that need or do they just know that I can do it? The purpose of a seminar is not to train every attendee on how every need can be solved. Attendees have their own needs. The purpose of the seminar is for them to decide whether or not you can help them. You either convince them that you can help them, or they convince you that you cannot help them. *(Continued on next page)*

(Ingredients to an ideal client seminar continued)

7. A question-and-answer period.

   Include a five-minute question-and-answer period at the end of your seminar presentation. Even if the most important client in the room has her hand up at the end of five minutes, do not answer her question, but tell her that you will after the seminar.

   Following the question-and-answer period, summarize some of the key issues mentioned during the presentation. After the summary, thank the audience and adjourn the meeting.

8. 48 hours

   Within 48 hours of the seminar (and no later than 72 hours), call every attendee. Thank each for attending. Tell them that the material they asked for on the seminar questionnaire has been complied. But since you have the person on the phone, ask him or her if there are any questions that you can answer. Then say,

   > "I am going to be in your area next week. When would be a convenient time to get together. Is Monday good or is Tuesday better?"

   The purpose of a seminar is to book appointments. Call every attendee and schedule an appointment. That is your "mission."

When should you expect your commissions from the seminar to exceed seminar expenses?

We tell many that commissions resulting from the seminar will always, always, always exceed seminar expenses. This is always true. The whole problem is when will commissions exceed seminar expenses? Will it take one week or will it take five years? Or, maybe even a lifetime? The precise date when commissions exceed seminar expenses is called "the crossover point."

Many people have asked me what is an acceptable crossover point. On the average, three to 12 months would be an acceptable crossover point. That may seem like a long time, but remember, after you have reached the crossover point, 100% of the commissions are "gravy." Your career will benefit if you do seminars the right way and if you do them frequently. Spend little and invite many.

4 additional seminar maxims to follow

1. Avoid special speakers.

    On the subject of speakers, we suggest that you do not have a special speaker when you are doing retail customer seminars, unless you are creating a 200-plus client seminar at a five-star hotel site. You should be the speaker. You want to be the authority figure. You want to be the answer person. But, if it's unavoidable, allow that other speaker to speak for only 15 or 20 minutes.
    (Continued on next page)

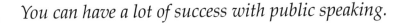

(4 additional seminar maxims to follow continued)

2. Hold your seminar mid-week.

   A Tuesday, Wednesday, or Thursday evening at about 7 p.m. Never do a seminar seven to ten days before or after a holiday.

3. Include wholesalers.

   Whenever possible, arrange for a wholesaler to have a table in the back of the seminar room. In return for being part of your seminar, the wholesaler will pay you anywhere from $100 to $300. Be sure to introduce the wholesaler at the end of the seminar and encourage the seminar attendees to visit the wholesaler's table. Remember, when you have a wholesaler, there must always be three winners. The audience must win. You must win. And, the wholesaler involved in your seminar must win as well.

4. Call people who have registered.

   Each person who has registered deserves a phone call from your staff the day before the seminar (not two or three days before) to remind them about the seminar and to again ask if they would like to bring a friend, family member, or neighbor to the seminar. The key to this confirmation is again reminding them of the benefits of attending. Tell them again what they will learn, what time it starts, what time it ends, and it is FREE.

   Remember, 80% of the people who R.S.V.P. at weddings show up. And if 80% of the people show up at weddings, it is your challenge to get close to 80% of the people to show up at your seminar. If you call those people and remind them of the benefits, it will make your seminar investment a much wiser one.

How to do a client seminar with no expenses

Contact the person in charge of selecting guest speakers for the Kiwanis, Rotary, Jaycees, Lions, etc., and offer your services to that group. You are a professional in the financial services industry. You can help their members.

Notice the opportunity that you are creating for yourself. You are being allowed to speak before a group of people. You do not have to mail invitations to any of the people who will be attending. You are having a seminar without renting a hotel site or community room, and, possibly, without renting any audio or visual equipment.

A review of the 7 sections of your seminar

1. Sign-In

2. Introduction
   Introduce yourself. Introduce what you do and how you help people. In this introductory phase of your seminar, make sure you emphasize your proximity and how you work closely with other professionals on behalf of your clients (if you do). Mention your degrees, if any, and your service philosophy.

3. The presentation
   Keep it visual and only 45 minutes long.

4. The questionnaire
   Earlier, we gave you an example of a seminar questionnaire that we urge you to hand out to attendees and have them complete during your seminar. These questions are not special. It is how you use the questionnaire that makes it special.

5. The question-and-answer period
   Keep it only 5 minutes long.

6. Adjourn and thank the audience for attending

7. Follow-up phone calls within 48 hours of the seminar

If you do many seminars, it does pay to own your own equipment. Make a minor investment and over a period of time, you will save yourself a great deal of money.

Catchy titles for your seminar

As discussed earlier, you should research the seminar topics which are being presented in your area. Then you should create a title that stands out from all of the others. For example, any of the following titles with the right seminar invitation would work in our area because no one is advertising them this way.

Two ways to avoid probate™

How to reduce taxes on Social Security income

24 questions to ask about every annuity before you buy it

Summary: In this secret, you learned

- 22 speaking tips to follow
- how to write the seminar invitation
- 4 things to do 6-8 weeks before your seminar
- what to do 90 minutes before the seminar
- 3 things you must do
- the ingredients to an ideal client seminar
- when you should expect your commissions from the seminar to exceed seminar expenses
- 4 additional seminar maxims to follow
- how to do a client seminar with no expenses
- the 7 sections of your seminar
- catchy titles for your seminar

5 *You can have a lot of success with public speaking.*

Public Speaking Quiz

1. With speaking publicly, you should

a) memorize your presentation
b) mimic the personality of another highly successful presenter
c) be yourself

2. All of the tips below are important EXCEPT

a) care about the audience
b) eye contact
c) visuals
d) humor

3. The things you must do are

a) be likeable
b) give them 2-3 unforgettable ideas
c) convince them they need you
d) all of the above

Answers: 1 c, 2 d, 3 d

6

You can have success with Leads.

L eads are opportunities, selling opportunities for you and buying opportunities for your prospect. In this secret, you'll learn how to multiply selling opportunities by learning how to contact leads acquired from a respected vendor by using the right attitude, phone scripts, and the right approaches.

6 *You can have success with Leads.*

Leads

We often compare leads to the four bases on a baseball diamond. First base leads are names in a telephone book. Second base leads are qualified leads you have purchased from a special vendor. Third base leads are referrals from a client. And, home plate represents your existing clients. In other words, a qualified lead is better than a name in a telephone book but not as good as a referral.

In baseball, the closer you are to home plate, the more apt you are to score. In the financial profession, the more time you spend with your clients, referrals and then qualified leads, the more apt you are to achieve a higher level of selling success. In the future, you should spend 60% of your time with clients and referrals. But, how you prospect the balance of the time will determine your real success.

By simply purchasing qualified leads from a highly respected vendor, you can save both money and time. And, the money that you save can be reinvested into other proven business building approaches like additional staffing. But, how much better is that qualified lead from a respected vendor than a name in a telephone book? Does that qualified lead become an "A" client with repeated business and referrals year after year after year? Or, is this lead from a vendor just a one-time phone call?

Surprisingly, the ultimate amount of business that you write from a "qualified lead" from a respected vendor is controlled by the steps and approaches that you use more so than how the lead was obtained from the vendor.

Here are 3 proven steps to follow when contacting leads (even referrals and clients).

Step #1: Your first step to converting a lead to a client starts with your attitude. Is that lead just a potential commission or is a lead a person whom you can help plan for retirement? A lead just being a commission may put money in your pocket today, but will not help you achieve long-term success. You must care about that lead to build a successful career.

Step #2: Your second step is that you should gravitate to a product or concept that motivates you. Is the lead expressing interest in a product that you believe in? Always gravitate toward a product, concept, or market that gets you motivated and purchase leads of people most apt to be interested in that product, concept, or market.

Step #3: Your first phone call should embrace 8 proven phone approaches. How many of these proven phone techniques do you currently use?

8 Proven phone approaches

1. Visualize success before picking up the phone.
2. Recall all of the benefits of working with you and the benefits of owning your product before picking up the phone.
3. Make the call standing up.
4. Have a genuine smile on your face when you call.
5. Do not ask questions that you do not know the answers to.
6. Know how to overcome phone objections. (please re-read our Using The Phone Secret)
7. Know how to keep a telephone relationship alive, even when you do not successfully overcome the objection.
8. Use a phone script that works.

6 *You can have success with Leads.*

In the following paragraphs, we provide a "wrong" phone approach followed by the right phone approach. More importantly, we will then dissect both approaches and examine why your NEW way of using the phone can help you achieve a level of success far beyond even your hopes and dreams.

Wrong Phone Approach

You: "Is this Mrs. Tucker?"

Lead: "Yes, it is."

You: "How are you?"

Lead: "Who are you?"

You: "I'm Bob Smith. How are you?"

Lead: "What do you want?"

You: "You have expressed interest in a product."

Lead: "No, I didn't."

You: "Yes, you did."

Lead: "No, I didn't."

You: "I can prove it to you, Mrs. Tucker."

Lead: "No, you can't."

You: "Oh, yes I can!!"

Lead: Goodbye!!!!!!!!!!!!!!!!!!!!!!!!!!

You :   Boy, that was a lousy lead.

Correct Phone Approach

You: "Mrs. Tucker?" (with a slight question in your voice)
Lead: "Yes, it is."

You: "You recently expressed interest in reducing income taxes on the interest you earn in the bank? I hope that I am contacting you at an okay time. Where would it be a convenient place to get together? We can meet at my office, or at coffee shop close to you, or at your place. Do you have a preference?"
Lead: "I cannot remember asking to be contacted." (or almost any objection)

You: "Sometimes we hear people say that, but we almost always hear that they want to (repeat benefit said earlier) reduce income taxes on the interest they earn at the bank. (now repeat close said earlier) We can meet at my office, or at coffee shop close to you, or at your place. Do you have a preference?"
Lead: "We really have no money to invest at this time."

You: "I can appreciate how you feel, however, the people that benefit the most from our services are those people who initially did not think that they had any money to invest. Where is the best place to discuss reducing income taxes on the interest you earn at the bank, my office, coffee shop close to you, or your place?"
Lead: "No thank you. This is really a terrible time. Our daughter is getting married this month."

You: "I can appreciate that. I can remember my wedding. Would you mind if I called you back in about 30 days when things might be a little better for you?"
Lead: "That would be fine."

You: "Have a nice day and a great wedding."
Lead: "Thanks for the nice words and you too."

(Continued on next page)

You can have success with Leads.

(Correct phone approach continued)

Note: Some of you might feel that even the second phone script was NOT successful, but it really was. One of the biggest mistakes that we make when making a phone call to a lead is the unnecessary pressure that we place on ourselves to succeed. If you do not schedule an appointment during that first phone call, so many of us think that we failed. And, we never call that lead back again. We make too many first time phone calls and not enough second (and third and fourth) phone calls. Effective immediately, whenever you get an objection that you cannot overcome, open the door to another phone call at a later date.

Or, said in a different way, a qualified lead is no more a guaranteed sale than a referral is from an existing client. Leads are just opportunities but sometimes GREAT opportunities.

However, let's dissect the scripts previously given and discover the pitfalls and strengths.

Wrong Script

"How are you?"

Never ask a question if you do not know the answer. You do not want to start a phone call with hearing about their recent visit to the dentist. Naturally, this advice does not apply to a phone call to a client or to a fellow associate.

"You expressed interest in an annuity"

We do not mind if you mention annuity in your phone call, but we do mind if you do not mention one of the many benefits to owning an annuity. People buy because of how the benefits sound to them, not because of how the word annuity sounds.

"No, I didn't. Yes, you did."

Never, never argue with a lead (or referral or client.)

The Correct Script

The correct script used popular proven techniques that make all of the sense in the world.

First, they heard one of the benefits within the first 5 seconds.

Second, they have a choice of places to meet you. If you were a widow, would you feel comfortable meeting a man that you have never met in the privacy of your home? The choice of places makes sense, doesn't it?

Third, their first objection was addressed by you repeating the benefit and repeating the close. "Sometimes we hear that but we always hear that people would like to reduce income taxes." You are not trying to be pushy, but you are trying to keep this telephone call lasting longer. After all, they just met you 10 seconds ago. Should we expect them to want to meet you after hearing the benefits only once?

Fourth, the next objection was .addressed by using the "benefit the most" words, a proven way for you to keep the relationship alive. "The people who benefit the most from our services were people who (now repeat their objection) initially thought that they had no money to set aside".

Lastly, and most importantly, you kept the relationship alive by seeking permission for you to contact them later. "Would you mind if I called you back when things might be a little better"?

Are All Leads Equal?

We use the words "leads "and "qualified leads "throughout this secret since there is a big difference between the two. Technically speaking, "a lead" could be defined as anyone expressing interest in a product in return for a gift like a road atlas, miniature flashlight or special coffee cup. While they are leads, they might NOT be the ideal lead since you might spend more time discussing or dropping off the gift than the benefits of owning an annuity. On the other hand, there are "qualified leads". They are NOT guaranteed sales but they are opportunities and some of them might be potentially great opportunities.

6

You can have success with Leads.

Are all lead providers equal?

Here are some of the questions you should ask.

Question 1

Once a prospect asks for an agent to contact them, how soon is the agent notified that there is a qualified lead?

Desired Answer: 4 hours - 24 hours

Question 2

What if the prospect turns out to be just a curious insurance agent and not a qualified lead?

Desired Answer: You get another lead at no additional charge.

Question 3

After the qualified lead is notified that an agent will be calling them, can the lead opt out and change their mind?

Desired Answer: Yes

In the future, 60% of our time should be spent with our existing clients and referrals. However, we must spend the balance of the time finding potential clients by using traditional proven prospecting techniques and unique innovative prospecting programs discussed in Secret 7. Unquestionably, leads from a respected vendor can enable you to achieve a higher level of selling success. However, so much of that success depends upon your attitude, how you really feel about the product, and your phone skills. But, just like a baseball player, success begins with practice. After all, all you need to achieve Hall of Fame status is fail 60% of the time. Ted Williams did it in 1946 and you can do it now!

Summary: In this secret, you learned

- 3 proven steps to follow when contacting leads

- the wrong phone approach

- the correct phone approach

- the correct script

- that all lead providers are not equal

6 *You can have success with Leads.*

Leads Quiz

1. Qualified Leads

a) can save you time and money
b) are opportunities
c) can be potential clients if you have the right attitude
d) all of the above

2. Leads success is often preceded by

a) knowing how to use the phone
b) discussing a product or concept that motivates you
c) you having the correct attitude
d) all of the above
e) the lead vendor carefully selecting the best leads

Answers: 1 d, 2 d

secret 7

You can triple your income by using some of these Prospecting Programs.

This book addresses 14 different ways to build your clientele. In the preceding pages, we discussed 4 proven traditional ways such as Using The Phone, Getting Referrals, Seminars, and Leads. On the following pages, we unveil 10 proven, unique, forgotten, or overlooked Prospecting Programs. You are one page away from potentially tripling your clientele and income. Do you want to turn the page?

You can triple your income by using some of these Prospecting Programs.

Did you ever watch the Ed Sullivan show and see this act where a man was attempting to spin 14 plates on 14 poles? He would first get one plate to spin. Then, he quickly moved to his right and got that second plate spinning, but frantically returned to the first plate right before it was about to crash onto the stage. Then, he rushed to the third plate to get that plate to spin before returning to the other 2 plates just in time. Eventually, he would have all 14 plates spinning. We are doing the same thing. However, we are not using "plates." We are using proven prospecting approaches. "Plate" #1 is using the phone. "Plate" #2 would be getting referrals and "Plates"#3-14 would be unique, proven, or forgotten prospecting programs discussed in this book.

If possible, one should try to do as many of these 14 prospecting approaches as possible. Surprisingly, only some of the prospecting approaches such as seminars, direct mail, and leads require an investment. A few others require a special skill like being a guest on TV. The other prospecting approaches are either FREE or almost FREE and are for almost everyone.

Before we discuss 10 more prospecting programs, allow me to
address one of the most important topics in this entire book.
And that topic is your existing clients. They are priceless,
invaluable, and they should never be given less priority or
attention than a prospective client. Said differently, you
know how hard it is to add a client to your clientele. Treasure
your clients. Give them pleasant buying experiences for two
reasons. First and most importantly, they deserve your best.
Second and more selfishly, your existing clients become a
source of repeated business and referrals year after year. As
mentioned earlier, we should spend 60% of our time with our
clients and referrals. However, 40% of our time must be spent
looking for, finding, and converting prospects into clients.

On the following pages, we discuss the following proven,
unique, forgotten, or often overlooked Prospecting Programs:

You can triple your income by using some of these Prospecting Programs.

**You are
one
page
away
from**

· · · learning how to use Online Birthday Marketing.

Prospecting Approach #1: Online Birthday Marketing

The Internet can help you make Birthday Marketing both relationship-building and sales-creating. W.V.H., Inc. has a Birthday Marketing web site: http://www.birthdaywebsite.net that is potentially award–winning since the web site gives YOU:

a) an easy way to:

   distinguish yourself in the eyes of the prospects,

   create more rapport with your clientele,

   discover the simplest needs–based presentation ever created

b) the freedom to personalize Birthday Web Sites and Birthday Certificates for your clientele and prospect pipeline in less than 30 seconds

c) an easy way to email links of the Birthday Web Site and Birthday Certificate to your clientele and prospect pipeline

d) an excellent training video on how you can maximize Birthday Marketing Success

e) FREE access and permission to print and mail up to 100 Birthday Newsletters every month (free access for subscribers only)

7

You can triple your income by using some of these Prospecting Programs.

However, our website is not the only way to succeed in Birthday Marketing. There are probably some other services that can give you the data that you need but carefully read their Terms/Conditions and Use sections at the bottom of their web sites first. Someone just recently lost $500,000 for using something that they were not allowed to use for business purposes. Our website DOES allow you to use it for prospecting, presenting, and over the phone.

As you see on the opposite page, our website www. birthdaywebsite.net allows subscribers to create and print Birthday Web Sites and Birthday Certificates for the point-of-sale, email links of the Birthday Web Sites and Birthday Certificates for telephone appointments, and print and mail Birthday Newsletters for a follow-up phone call. Or, you can do all of the above because you just want to be unforgettable. More importantly, because you care.

Subscribers simply go to this web site*, log in, and

• create Birthday Web Sites and Certificates

• email links of Web Sites and Certificates

• print Birthday Newsletters

*www.birthdaywebsite.net

7

You can triple your income by using some of these Prospecting Programs.

How to Use Birthday Marketing

Strategy #1a Use Our **Birthday Web Sites** As The Reason To Schedule Appointments Over The Phone:

Birthday Marketing becomes a great "excuse" to contact 2 existing clients, former clients, and current prospects every day since you can now customize a Web Site for them based on the day they were born. And it will take you only 30 seconds to customize a Web Site!

Naturally, using your own personality and your own words, say something like:

> "Joe, this is (your name). I just created a web site about you and the day that you were born.(using your passion in your voice) You've got to see it. Where is the best place to get together for 15 minutes, your place, my place, or at your favorite coffee shop?"

They will like seeing what things cost the day they were born and they will love watching the videos to what was happening the day they were born–even if their birthday is months away. Birthday Marketing makes outbound calling fun. Suggestion: Since it only takes 30 seconds for you to create a personalized web site, create the web site first. Then call. We all need passion in our voice and the unforgettable insurance and financial-related items that appear on their Birthday Web Site will give us the sincere passion that we all need over the phone.

On the opposite page is an example of a Multi-Media website that you can create for any client or prospect in 30 seconds. 30 seconds? Yes, subscribers just visit www.birthdaywebsite.net, enter their client's or prospect's name and date of birth, click submit, and your client's or prospect's website appears in seconds.

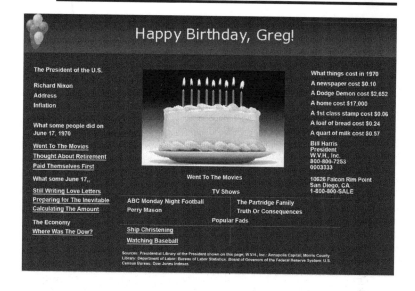

Happy Birthday, Greg!

The President of the U.S.

Richard Nixon
Address
Inflation

What some people did on
June 17, 1970

Went To The Movies
Thought About Retirement
Paid Themselves First

What some June 17,.

Still Writing Love Letters
Preparing for The Inevitable
Calculating The Amount

The Economy
Where Was The Dow?

What things cost in 1970
A newspaper cost $0.10
A Dodge Demon cost $2,652
A home cost $17,000
A 1st class stamp cost $0.06
A loaf of bread cost $0.24
A quart of milk cost $0.57

Bill Harris
President
W.V.H., Inc.
800-800-7253
0003333

10626 Falcon Rim Point
San Diego, CA
1-800-800-SALE

Went To The Movies

TV Shows

ABC Monday Night Football
Perry Mason

The Partridge Family
Truth Or Consequences

Popular Fads

Ship Christening

Watching Baseball

Sources: Presidential Library of the President shown on this page; W.V.H., Inc.: Annapolis Capital; Morris County Library: Department of Labor: Bureau of Labor Statistics: Board of Govenors of the Federal Reserve System: U.S. Census Bureau; Dow Jones Indexes.

Each web site has 4 important sections

Top Banner : Their Name
Right : What Things Cost
Lower Right : Your Contact Information
Left : 6 Insurance Related Videos

You can triple your income by using some of these Prospecting Programs.

Strategy #1b Use Our **Birthday Web Sites** At The Point-of-Sale With The Appointments You Have Scheduled

If you do not use a computer at the point-of-sale, you can print the birthday website in full color before the appointment. During the appointment, you can take out the printout and discuss what things cost the day they were born using our proven inflation-fighting script. Or, by using your computer or theirs, you can show any 1 of the 6 unforgettable videos that are on their website. If they are more than 99 miles away, schedule a telephone appointment with them first, email a link of the website to them, and have your appointment with them over the phone. However, make sure you are licensed in that state.

You can discuss what things cost by pointing to the far right hand side of their website (see previous page) and use our inflation fighting script on the following page.

(Continued on next page)

(Strategy # 1b Use Our Birthday Web Sites At The Point-of-Sale With The Appointments You Have Scheduled continued)

Inflation-fighting script:

"Greg, in 1970, the year that you were born. A newspaper cost 10 cents. A first class stamp cost 6 cents. A brand new Dodge Demon cost $2,652. And, a home in some sections of the country cost $17,000.

Question #1: "Do you think that a newspaper, car, and a home will cost more 10 years from now than they do today? Everyone says "Yes!"

Question #2: "What are you doing about this problem of yours?" And, after they say, "Nothing," or just shrug their shoulders, ask question #3.

Question #3: "Would you like me to show you how to potentially lessen the impact that inflation can have on your retirement dollars?"

WOW!!!! You now know the easiest, best and simplest way to return to needs-based selling. Simply use what things cost the day they were born and ask 3 questions that took us a career to learn, refine and master. *(Continued on next page)*

You can triple your income by using some of these Prospecting Programs.

(Strategy # 1b Use Our Birthday Web Sites At The Point-of-Sale With The Appointments You Have Scheduled Continued)

Another real special way to use **Birthday Web Sites** is to show 1 of the 6 insurance related videos that are on every Birthday Web Site website that you create. (assuming that you elect the video option when you become a subscriber) Which videos should you play at the point-of sale? First, only show one or two videos at the max since you are not supposed to be a movie theatre. You are supposed to be a Solutionist.

Which videos are sales-creating? Using the opposite page as a road map:

1. To show the devastating impact of inflation and the importance of having more money later. Play "Went To The Movies"

2. To show the importance of you helping them. Play "Thought About Retirement"

3. To show people the importance of beginning to save Play "Paid Themselves First"

Want to sell more life insurance this year than ever before?

4. Play "Still Writing Love Letters". Arguably the best life insurance film of all time.

5. Play "Preparing For The Inevitable" if you want to discuss getting things in order for the surviving spouse.

6. Play "Calculating The Amount" if you want to discuss the best way to calculate how much life insurance is enough.

Want to have fun?

• Click on the links under "the President of the United States" if you want to smile plus click on the link "Where Was The Dow?" if you want to laugh since it shows how well the stock market has done since their DOB.

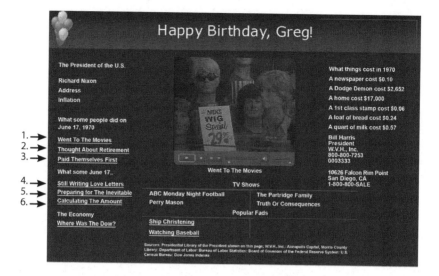

1. → Went To The Movies
2. → Thought About Retirement
3. → Paid Themselves First

4. → Still Writing Love Letters
5. → Preparing for The Inevitable
6. → Calculating The Amount

1. Discuss the impact of inflation

2. Talk about thinking about their money

3. Show the importance of saving

4. Unveil the real purpose of life insurance

5. Review how to prepare

6. Introduce Human Life Value

7 *You can triple your income by using some of these Prospecting Programs.*

Strategy #2a Use Our **Birthday Certificates** Over The Phone To Schedule Appointments

Birthday Marketing becomes a great "excuse" to contact 2 existing clients, current prospects, and referrals every day since you can also create a Birthday Certificate based on the day they were born. Naturally, using your own personality and your own words, say something like:

"Joe, this is (your name). I just created a Birthday Certificate about you and the day that you were born.(using your passion in your voice) You've got to see it. Where is the best place to get together for 15 minutes, your place, my place, or at your favorite coffee shop?"

They will like seeing what things cost-even if their birthday is months away. Birthday Marketing makes outbound calling fun. Suggestion: Since it only takes 30 seconds for you to create a personalized Birthday Certificate, create the Birthday Certificate first. Then call. We all need passion in our voice and the sales-creating section devoted to what things cost and the unforgettable section devoted to what % of people had a telephone, radio, TV or cable TV just makes earning money a lot of fun.

On the opposite page is an example of a Birthday Certificate that I created in 30 seconds. 30 seconds? Yes, subscribers just visit www.birthdaywebsite.net, enter your client's or prospect's name and date of birth, click submit, and the Birthday Certificate appears—ready to print—in seconds.

Birthday Certificate

For

Greg Jones

June 17, 1970

Interesting facts	What things cost
President: Richard Nixon	A newspaper cost $0.10
Life Expectancy:	A Dodge Demon cost $2,652
Male: 67.1; Female: 74.7	A home cost $17,000
CD Interest Rate: 7.64%	A 1st class stamp cost $0.06
% of Households With:	A loaf of bread cost $0.24
Telephone: 90.5%	A ½ gallon of milk cost $0.57
Radio: 99%	
TV: 95.3%	
Cable TV: 6.7%	

800-800-7253

10026 Falcon Run Point
San Diego,CA
1-800-800-SALE

Bill Harris, President
W.V.H., Inc.

Sources: Nixon Presidential Library, W.V.H. Inc., Annapolis Capital, Morris County Library, Department of Labor, Bureau of Labor Statistics, Board of Governors of the Federal Reserve System, U.S. Census Bureau

See reverse side for disclosure.

Each Birthday Certificate Has 6 Important Sections:

Top Center : Their Name and Date of Birth
Prominently Displayed

Right : What Things Cost

Bottom Right : Gorgeous Gold Seal

Left : Who Was President
Life Expectancy
Interest Rates
% of Households Who Had
Phone, Radio, TV

Bottom Left : Your Contact Information

Bottom Center : Space For Your Signature

7 *You can triple your income by using some of these Prospecting Programs.*

Strategy #2b Using Our **Birthday Certificates** At The End of Every Appointment

Every morning, create a Birthday Certificate for everyone you are seeing that day. Any prospect. Any client. Any former client.

Following your presentation, annual review, service call, or policy delivery, please say,

"Oh, by the way, early this morning, I created a Birthday Certificate for you that is based upon the day you were born. May I show it to you?"

Friends, how many will say, "No, I do not want to see this Birthday Certificate that is all about me!" Everyone will want to see it. Then, take out the Birthday Certificate that you created but make sure you have not signed your name to it yet. (see previous page for unsigned Birthday Certificate). And say the following words. Why? Because they work!

"Greg, in 1970, the year that you were born. A newspaper cost 10 cents. A first class stamp cost 6 cents. And, a home in some sections of the country cost $17,000.

Question #1: "Do you think that a newspaper, postage, and home will cost more 10 years from now than they do today?" Everyone says "Yes!"

Question #2: "What are you doing about this problem of yours?" And, after they say, "Nothing," or just shrug their shoulders, ask

Question #3: "Would you like me to show you how to potentially lessen the impact that inflation can have on your retirement dollars?"

Then show them how an annuity can help and then say, "May I sign your Birthday Certificate that I created for you?" Then close.

You
are
1
page
away
from.

. . . learning what to do right before their birthday.

You can triple your income by using some of these Prospecting Programs.

Strategy #2c Use Our **Birthday Certificates** Right Before Their Birthday

As you will learn on page 189, your file cabinet is a gold mine of leads since it has every application you have ever taken and every illustration or proposal you ever presented. Said differently, you have the dates of birth of every client, every former client, and every current prospect. A GOLD MINE!

A few days before their birthday. Call everyone who is about to have a Birthday and use the following words Why? Because they work.

"Max, this is Bill Harris and I know that your Birthday is coming up and I have a small gift to give you. Where and when can I give it to you? How about the day before your birthday at your favorite ice cream shop? (pause for response; if no response quickly say) How about your place or at Starbucks? You'll love this small gift."

Do you know anyone who is going to say that they do not want your small gift? After they say "Yes", print a Birthday Certificate, sign it, grab $1.99 or 3.99 and go to WalMart and buy a picture frame, and put the signed Birthday Certificate into the frame. (please see opposite page)

Since I cannot even put a light bulb in, Mrs. H. puts the Certificate in the frame. And, you know something, when I visit my clients who are senior officers of insurance companies and Marketing Organizations, almost all of them have their framed Birthday Certificate on their office walls, along with very expensive art, memorabilia, etc.

Friends, it does not take much to be unforgettable! But you know something, I did NOT do it to be unforgettable or to almost guarantee a future sale. I did it because I really like the people for whom I created Birthday Certificates.

"Do your clients think of you every year on their birthday? They soon will."

You can triple your income by using some of these Prospecting Programs.

Strategy #3 Use Our **Birthday Emails** With Any Client, Former Client, and Current Prospect More Than 99 Miles Away

There will never be any email as powerful as you "in person". As a result, it might only make sense to use the email part of our Birthday Marketing program for clients more than 99 miles away. After you register as a subscriber and elect the email part of the program, you can send an email with the links of Birthday Web Site and Birthday Certificate. On the opposite page, we show the email. Keep the email as is or you can amend any of the words.

Send E-Mail

To: [_____]

Reply-To: Your email address goes here

Subject: [When you were born _____]

Dear Bill,

We have created a Multi-media web site and Birthday Certificate about you and the day that you were born.

Simply click on the links below. If you have 2 minutes, look at the videos on the left hand side of your web site.

Many of the videos are all about the day you were born.

To see your new web site, click on the link below.

http://www.birthdaywebsite.net/view_pdf_web.php?prdID2=9711&md5=fa658df9edd7f49d31756df9791c22

To see and print your Birthday Certificate, you can click on the link below.

http://www.birthdaywebsite.net/view_pdf_web.php?prdID=9712&md5=fa658df9edd7f49d31756df9791c22

Your Birthday Certificate will look great in a picture frame.

Your Name

You can triple your income by using some of these Prospecting Programs.

Strategy #4 Use Our **Virtual File Cabinet** To Save All Birthday Web Sites, Birthday Certificates, Birthday Emails

Since record keeping is essential to every professional, current subscribers have lightening speed access to every Birthday Web Site, Birthday Certificate, Birthday Email created. This Virtual File Cabinet is invaluable. Instead of driving to the pharmacy to get a birthday card every year, just return to your Virtual File cabinet on www.birthdaywebsite.net to retrieve Birthday Web Sites and Birthday Certificates already created by you. And Birthday Emails too. And, you have access to the **Virtual File Cabinet** as long as you are a subscriber.

Your new virtual file cabinet

BIRTHDAY MARKETING

My Certificates, Websites, Cards, and Videos

Display My Certificates, Websites, Cards, and Videos for... | View all | ▼ | View

Search by Client's Name: [_____] | Search | All

Date/Time	Client's Name	PDF	WEB	Mail
Wed, Jul 28, 2010 - 12:35:28 PM	Bill Harris	PDF	WEB	Mail
Tue, Jun 22, 2010 - 12:36:12 PM	Wayne Harrison	PDF	WEB	Mail
Wed, May 26, 2010 - 08:16:59 AM	Tanya Brown	PDF	WEB	Mail
Wed, May 26, 2010 - 07:20:22 AM	Jor Rich	PDF	WEB	Mail
Tue, May 25, 2010 - 10:50:59 AM	James Robbins	PDF	WEB	Mail
Tue, May 25, 2010 - 08:14:36 AM	Bill Harris	PDF	WEB	Mail
Mon, May 24, 2010 - 01:43:40 PM	James M.Richards	PDF	WEB	Mail
Mon, May 24, 2010 - 12:46:35 PM	Jim Stevens	PDF	WEB	Mail
Fri, May 21, 2010 - 01:16:48 PM	Shelly Sas	PDF	WEB	Mail
Fri, May 21, 2010 - 01:16:43 PM	Shelly Williams	PDF	WEB	Mail
Fri, May 21, 2010 - 01:14:29 PM	Jim Martin	PDF	WEB	Mail
Fri, May 21, 2010 - 01:13:59 PM	Jane Raster	PDF	WEB	Mail
Fri, May 21, 2010 - 01:09:51 PM	Sandy johnson	PDF	WEB	Mail
Fri, May 21, 2010 - 01:09:50 PM	Bob o Reilly	PDF	WEB	Mail
Fri, May 21, 2010 - 01:02:19 PM	Dave Speck	PDF	WEB	Mail
Fri, Apr 2, 2010 - 10:55:00 AM	Steve Peck	PDF	WEB	Mail
Sat, Feb 20, 2010 - 05:00:27 PM	Charles Gerber	PDF	WEB	Mail
Sat, Feb 6, 2010 - 02:15:31 PM	Joan Catalano	PDF	WEB	Mail
Mon, Feb 1, 2010 - 11:47:11 AM	Barry Councilman	PDF	WEB	Mail
Mon, Feb 1, 2010 - 11:47:04 AM	Mary Counce	PDF	WEB	Mail
Wed, Jan 13, 2010 - 08:44:19 AM	Dave Dole	PDF	WEB	Mail
Fri, Jan 8, 2010 - 09:17:15 AM	Pete Bolitta	PDF	WEB	Mail
Fri, Jan 8, 2010 - 05:38:30 AM	Anthony Berretto	PDF	WEB	Mail
Sat, Oct 10, 2009 - 04:56:25 PM	Ronand Coluck	PDF	WEB	Mail
Sat, Oct 10, 2009 - 04:53:29 PM	Mary Broker	PDF	WEB	Mail
Sat, Oct 10, 2009 - 04:53:00 PM	Mary Dayton	PDF	WEB	Mail
Sat, Oct 10, 2009 - 04:52:31 PM	Homer Bedford	PDF	WEB	Mail
Sat, Oct 10, 2009 - 04:51:52 PM	Don Migliacco	PDF	WEB	Mail
Sat, Oct 10, 2009 - 04:46:17 PM	Dick Moore	PDF	WEB	Mail

. . . gives you lightening speed access to your Web Sites, Certificates, and Emails.

You can triple your income by using some of these Prospecting Programs.

Strategy #5 Use our **FREE Birthday Newsletters** With Any Client, Former Client, And Current Prospect

If you are a subscriber, even if it is just for the Birthday Certificate and nothing else, you can print and mail up to 100 Birthday Newsletters every month. We have one for every month of the year. So, in other words, you group your clientele according to the month they were born and mail accordingly. What makes our Birthday Newsletters so special? They are 1 page. The front of the Birthday Newsletter talks about a different topic each month such as inflation, tax deferral, retirement, etc. The back side is entertaining since it lists the most interesting things that happened in history during the month that they were born such as Famous Celebrity Birthdays, Famous Movies That Premiered That Month, and Famous Historical Events.

On the opposite page, we show the front of our September Newsletter.

Other Ways Of Using Our Birthday Newsletters:

1. Paperclip your business card to the newsletter and mail

2. Put the non-folded newsletter in a large birthday-like envelope and mail

3. Email PDF of newsletter instead of mailing

4. Have all 12 newsletters "standing up" at your client seminar registration table

5. Have all 12 newsletters with you and use the appropriate one at the point-of-sale

Happy Birthday

September Babies Are Unique!

September

For many September babies, rooting for your birthday to arrive was like wanting school to begin and summer to end. As result, many September babies learned how to mix pleasure (Birthday gifts) with pain (homework) and have done very well for themselves (please see famous September babies column on page 2). Recently, September babies- as well as babies from the other 11 months- have been living longer....much longer. As result, we have chosen to include a script that we wrote for a very short film titled Thinking About Retirement. We trust that you find the script informative and hope that it will encourage you to think about your retirement. By the way, Happy Birthday!

Thinking About Retirement

In 1950, the average man lived to age 65.6, a woman to age 71.1. Today, some men and women are running the marathon at that "young" age. In 1950, men and women worked and saved for 45 years for a 10-year retirement. Today, your retirement may last 40 years. In the past, risk to principal was a major concern. Today, outliving your money is becoming a bigger concern. As a result, there are a variety of products and concepts that can potentially help you prepare for retirement. The choice is yours. So, whether you want to play music, or dance to it, bicycle, or teach someone else, or just be a kid again, think about your money and your retirement on a regular basis. If you do, you are more apt to diversify, consider qualified and non-qualified retirement plans, pay yourself first, act cautiously, and stay out of debt.

Source: U.S. Census Bureau

> *In the past, risk to principal was a major concern.*
>
> ● ● ●
>
> *Today, outliving your money is becoming a bigger concern.*

North By Northwest with Cary Grant, Eva Marie Saint *and* **GoodFellas** with Robert DeNiro, Ray Liotta, *both premiered in September.*

See more September films on Page 2!

September 8, 1945
Son of Harris The Roofer

Car of the Month

1957 Chevy BelAire

Frankie Avalon, *is 68 this Sept. 18. Learn who else was born the same month as you on page 2!*

7 *You can triple your income by using some of these Prospecting Programs.*

THE INVESTMENT

Currently, your investment for our Birthday Marketing is unbelievably affordable since for as little as $2–$6 per week, your career can be enhanced. Maybe, your life can be changed.

The investment depends upon what you want. If you want to create:

- up to ten Birthday Certificates each week ($2 per week)

- up to ten Birthday Web Sites with unforgettable videos about the day they were born and ten Birthday Certificates ($4 per week)

- up to ten Birthday Emails, ten Birthday Certificates, and ten Birthday Web Sites with unforgettable videos about the day they were born ($6 per week)

- And you can terminate at any time so your investment to try out this career-changing approach is only $2-$6.

SUMMARY

After you have shown clients and prospects what a newspaper, new car, and a home cost the day that they were born from either the Birthday Web Site or Birthday Certificate, simply ask these 3 simple questions:

Question #1: "Do you think that a newspaper, car, and home will cost more 10 years from now than they do today?

Question #2: "What are you doing about this problem?" And, after they say, "Nothing," or just shrug their shoulders, ask

Question #3: "Would you like me to show you how to potentially lessen the impact that inflation can have on your retirement dollars?"

Then, show them how an annuity can help them accumulate more money.

Birthday Certificates and Birthday Web Sites about the day that they were born allow you to return to needs–based selling. As a result, your life and the lives of your clients can be enriched.

secret **7**

Prospecting Approach #2:
Consumer Webinars

When did you attend your first web conference? This year? Last year? In 2005? If it was 2005, did you know that the average web conference got only 33 RSVPs with only 8 - 12 insurance and investment professionals actually attending? However, things have changed. For example, one web conference that we do each month now gets almost 1,000 RSVPs with over 600 of them attending. While not every marketing organization or insurance company is getting those numbers, almost everyone has seen their web conference attendance skyrocket over the last 5 years.

Without a doubt, web conferencing is the most convenient and least expensive way for insurance and investment professionals to learn. Come to think of it, web conferencing may—suddenly—become the easiest, most convenient, and least expensive way for insurance and investment professionals to present. And as you will soon see, you will now be able to give a live annuity, life, or health insurance presentation to hundreds of prospects, and maybe to eventually thousands of prospects at the same time in the comfort of your home or office. The more I think about it, prospects can now listen to your presentation while in pajamas at home.

Are you willing, able, and capable of becoming a pioneer in Consumer Webinars if it enabled you to double or triple your clientele? If so, please read on.

7 *You can triple your income by using some of these Prospecting Programs.*

What is a webinar?

Wikipedia defines a webinar "as a specific type of web conference. It is typically one-way, from the speaker to the audience with limited audience interaction, such as in a webcast. A webinar can be collaborative and include polling and question & answer sessions to allow full participation between the audience and the presenter. In some cases, the presenter may speak over a standard telephone line, while pointing out information being presented on screen, and the audience can respond over their own telephones, speaker phones allowing the greatest comfort and convenience. There are web conferencing technologies on the market that have incorporated the use of audio technology, to allow for a completely web-based communication. Depending upon the provider, webinars may provide hidden or anonymous participant functionality, making participants unaware of other participants in the same meeting".

Three types of LIVE web conferences

1. Teleconference: Using the phone, you speak, they listen. They do not see anything.

   Advantages: Simplicity, lowest cost.

   Disadvantage: Since people retain information 22 times longer if they "see" and hear it, they retain less information with teleconferences. *(Continued on next page)*

(Three types of LIVE web conferences continued)

2. Web conference: Using the phone and a computer, you speak, they listen over the phone and they watch your presentation on their computer screen.

Advantage: They learn faster and retain more since they are both seeing and hearing it.

Disadvantage: Historically, the cost of this type of web conference has been much higher but that has already begun to change.

3. Hybrid: Using the phone and a computer, you speak and they listen over the phone and they visit your website where your presentation appears.

Advantages: Lower cost than a web conference.
They learn more than in a teleconference.

Disadvantage: This type of webinar has not "yet" been thoroughly tested. However, we are testing it now with some of our Consumer Webinars.

You can triple your income by using some of these Prospecting Programs.

Who should present?

Before we discuss who should present, let's examine the choices that you will soon have. You can be the presenter. Your insurance company, Broker-Dealer, or marketing organization can be the presenter. Or, an author can be the presenter.

An author as a presenter?

While it will probably change soon, to the best of our knowledge—as of August 3rd, 2010—we are the only author doing CONSUMER WEBINARS where insurance and investment professionals invite their prospects to listen to a generic presentation about saving for retirement. We are also the only ones who have created a library of email invitations, a pre-approach letter, and a direct mailer so insurance and investment professionals can effectively invite up to 35 clients, former clients, and current annuity prospects to attend.

Email this to your prospects.

You invite them.

We convince them.

Bill Harris, industry legend and author, unveils secrets about your money You need to listen and act before it is too late!

Live! Sorry no recording allowed

Listen to a live conference phone call with author Bill Harris at home!

Learn how to accumulate money with unnecessary risk in 20 Minutes! FREE! In the convenience of your home! With no obligation!

Let's talk soon.
I can only give away the toll-free number, date, and time of the call to a handful.

You will learn the following 3 Secrets from Bill's new book,
75 Secrets: An Insider's Guide to Bank CDs, Annuities, and Retirement Planning

- **Secret #34** Think about your money on a regular basis.
- **Secret #45** There are 5 risks far more devastating than risk to principal.
- **Secret # 40** There is an easy way to compute what your advisors are worth to you

"We owe it to our spouse, children, and grandchildren to be the best we can be. And, learning proven approaches, overlooked concepts, and forgotten strategies about accumulating more money for and during retirement is one example of you trying your best." **Bill Harris, president, W.V.H., Inc**

Learn what you need to know before it is too late.

The conference call is not investment, legal or tax advice. On the other hand, this conference call is a suggestion that you should think about your money on a regular basis and you should consult with your own advisors since what is best for you depends upon your circumstances. W.V.H., Inc and its officers and its employees do not recommend or endorse any insurance or investment professional, tax or legal advisor, insurance company or bank, or any company or anyone. W.V.H., Inc and its officers and its employees shall not be liable for any damages arising from any content discussed during this call and or any content in our book or on how anyone uses our book in whole or in part.

You can triple your income by using some of these Prospecting Programs.

Our Consumer Webinars

1. We have created a library of various ways that insurance and investment professionals can invite prospects to our Consumer Webinars where we speak. We have email invitations, a pre-approach letter for your letterhead, and a direct mailer (a postcard) for your printer. Currently, our plan is to do 8 free consumer webinars during the month of August and, maybe 1 consumer webinar every 3 months for insurance and investment professionals who own our *75 Secrets* book. They are free to those who own that book and they are free to the consumers. Our "internal" tag line is: *"You invite them. We convince them."*

And, as I write this part of the book, on August 16, 2010, we have done four consumer webinars. Our current feeling is this could be the greatest gift that any author, marketing organization, Broker/Dealer, or insurance company can do for any insurance or investment professional.

Said in a much different way, what better thing could one do than help an insurance and investment professional convert a prospect into a client? *(Continued on next page)*

**Allow
an
author
to
convince
your
prospects**

·
·
·
·
·
·
·
·
·
·
·

· · · while you are at the beach.

You can triple your income by using some of these Prospecting Programs.

(Our Consumer Webinars continued)

2. We recommend to our clients that they reach out to any annuity prospect whom they have already given an annuity presentation to on 2 or 3 occasions by using our email invitations (page 163), letter (see opposite page), direct mailer, or by using the carefully written words on the invitations or letter over the phone. We suggest that they schedule an appointment during the time of our webinar.

3. We then recommend that they reach out to other annuity prospects whom they have given their presentation to once and also invite them to attend the consumer webinar. However, we suggest scheduling an appointment with them one to four days after the consumer webinar.

To summarize so far, you make one appointment to listen to the consumer webinar with a prospect. You also make, for example, 16 appointments after the Consumer Webinar. You now have 17 appointments scheduled; one on the day of the webinar; 16 after the webinar.

Will you get 17 new clients as a result of 1 consumer webinar? No, you will not get anywhere close to 17 new clients but what if you get "only" 5 new annuity clients. If the average annuity premium is $50,000, you will have written one quarter of a million dollars of annuity premium where your investment in the Consumer Webinar was zero. (other than the $75 to get the *75 Secrets* book). However, you are not buying the book for free Consumer Webinars, you are investing in a $75 book so you can help your clients every day of the year.

(Continued on next page)

Put this on your letterhead and

Dear

I have made just arrangements so that my clients and prospective clients can learn and benefit from an industry legend and author, Bill Harris, President of W.V.H.,Inc.

Bill has just written a highly informative book that unveils how to accumulate more money for retirement by using proven approaches, overlooked concepts, and forgotten strategies. The book is titled 75 Secrets: An Insider's Guide To Bank CDs Annuities, and Retirement Planning.

To make a long story short, Bill will be having a live conference call EXCLUSIVELY for the clients and prospective clients of insurance professionals and investment professionals who bought the Advanced Copy of Bill's book before it arrives in bookstores.

The conference call is:

- FREE to you (I have already made the investment so you can listen for free)

- LIVE

- Only 20 minutes

- Convenient since you can listen at home   of this event.

- Very informative but you will need both your phone and your computer

There is no obligation but please listen since there will be NO RECORDING.

Sincerely,

Your Name
Your Title

P.S. You do NOT have to buy his $75 book since I did. I will show it to you. It can change how you live during retirement.

. . . mail to your clients & prospects. Then call them .

7

You can triple your income by using some of these Prospecting Programs.

(Our Consumer Webinars continued)

Use Online Intelligence

Have you ever asked a prospect to watch a TV show about, for example, retirement or have you asked them to read an article about, for example, long term care? Then, you asked them a question you did not know the answer to like,

> "Did you watch the show? Or "Did you have a chance to read the article?"

And you often heard, "No, I did not have the chance."

Would you like a better way?

In our Consumer Webinar library, we added a special announcement that will look great on your letterhead where it outlines the benefits of attending, date, times, toll free number. It also has the important web site address that they should visit a few minutes before they attend so that they can follow along and see the Secrets that we are unveiling. For your convenience, it is on the opposite page.

When they arrive at the site, W.V.H., Inc. created a really neat sign-in where they simply enter their name and the insurance and investment professional who invited them. Why is this sign-up so important? Immediately after the consumer webinar, we will send you an email telling you all of your prospects who attended. In other words, you now know which prospects are more apt to say, "YES!"

We only ask their name. In other words, we do NOT ask for mailing address or their email address. We get their name and who invited them such as YOU. *(Continued on next page)*

Put this on your letterhead

You are cordially invited to listen to a special live conference call with industry legend and author Bill Harris, President, W.V.H.,Inc.

Topic : How To Potentially Accumulate More Money For Retirement
    (and during retirement too)

What will you learn in 20 minutes:

1. Why you should think about your money on a regular basis plus who should be with you.
2. The 5 risks most frequently overlooked by savers and investors.
3. How to compute what your advisors are worth to you .

Cost to you: FREE: I have made an investment for a certain # of my guests to listen for FREE
Obligation: None at all. I am glad to help.
Recording: None so please listen and learn what few know.

Date :   August 3rd

Times: 11:30AM eastern with Encore at 7:30PM eastern

Toll free # :   1-800-XXX-XXXX

PIN: XXXXXX

Website Address For   http://signup.75secrets.com
August 3rd call:

Glad to help!

Your Name

> ### After the Consumer Webinar, we send you an email with the names of all of your prospects who attended.

You can triple your income by using some of these Prospecting Programs.

(Our consumer webinar continued)

Assuming that our book owners tell us their success stories, we will learn which of our material is most appropriate and most convincing. However, we are proud of the 3 Secrets that we are currently unveiling now from our *75 Secrets* book.

The first secret we unveil at our Consumer Webinar is Secret #34, *Think About Your Money on a Quarterly Basis*.

We thought this would be a terrific way to start off because it sets the stage when we say,

"So many of us do not think of our money on a regular basis. And, that is what insurance and investment professionals do best when they get together with you. They help you think about your money on a regular basis If you thought about your money, would you really owe $2,000 to VISA, American Express, paying interest rates of 18% to 22% when so many of you have $2,000 tucked away in the bank earning one-half of one percent. If you thought about your money on a regular basis, what would you do? You would go to the bank, withdraw that $2,000 at the bank earning one-half of one percent, and pay off the $2,000 credit card debt and immediately be 18% richer. But, so many of us don't do that because we don't think about our money regularly.

"When we were all growing up, our Dads and Moms always told us to never put all of our eggs in one basket. In spite of that, too many of us still do. So, beginning today, you must think about your money on a regular basis. And, the best person to think about your money on a regular basis is with your advisors and your insurance and investment professional. The bottom line is that we owe it to our spouse, to our children, and some of us also owe it to our grandchildren to be the best we can be and thinking about our money regularly is our job."

The second secret we unveil at our Consumer Webinars is Secret # 45: *The 5 Risks That Potentially Are More Devastating Than the Risk to Principal.*

We then review those 5 risks. While space does not allow us to elaborate on each of these risks, the 5 risks are inflation, income taxes, the lack of diversification, living longer, and Social Security.

The third secret is Secret #40. *There is an easy way to compute what your advisors are worth to you.*

This is a positive secret that shares the unbelievable value of an insurance and investment professional.

How To Increase Retention 22 times Longer

As reported earlier, consumers and insurance and investment professionals alike retain information 22 times longer if they both see it and hear it. With our Consumer Webinars, the audience sees each of these 3 secrets in an abridged version of an online book that we created specifically for these consumer webinars. In fact, you might be able to see it now by visiting www.75secrets.com *(continued on next page)*

7

You can triple your income by using some of these Prospecting Programs.

(Our consumer webinar continued)

Our Ending

We currently end our 15-20 minute Consumer Webinar with Secret #31: The importance of surrounding themselves with mentors who are willing, able, and capable of helping them achieve the financial and emotional independence they want and deserve. In other words, they need to surround themselves with an insurance and investment professional who is willing to meet with them and their other advisors regularly where they are the only topic and focus.

The CLOSE

We then thank the audience for attending and gently hang up the phone. As the call ends, insurance and investment professionals across America who are sitting with that prospect of theirs is ideally saying,

"Well, would you like to go ahead with it?"

Imagine
35 of your
annuity
prospects
learning
about
the
benefits
of owning
an
annuity

.
.
.
.
.

. . . while relaxed at home.

You can triple your income by using some of these Prospecting Programs.

An insurance company, Broker-Dealer, or marketing organization being the consumer webinar presenter?

Soon, insurance companies, Broker-Dealers, and marketing organizations will probably enter the CONSUMER WEBINAR arena since they know that the single best thing they can do for an insurance and investment professional is to help them convert a prospect into a client. Hopefully, they will ask us to help them. We feel that our "process" is so unique, we are filing papers to get a Patent Pending.

You as a presenter?

Without a doubt, you should be the presenter—not some author or some "executive" if:

> you love presenting over the phone

> you have the patience to wait for attendance to skyrocket

> you have the right strategic partners (web conference and phone vendors)

> you have marketing and prospecting dollars to invest; otherwise, use an author, insurance company, Broker-Dealer, or marketing organization since consumer webinars can be FREE.

secret **7**

Should the webinar be live or should it be recorded?

Both have its advantages. However, as a presenter, I love the live webinar since I can weave current, relevant information into my presentation. Just yesterday, less than 15 minutes before my 7:30 PM consumer webinar, I read an email from one of our book owners requesting that we mention Secret *#69 Forget About Recovering Your 2008 Losses Quickly.* Minutes later, everyone heard me make a reference to that Secret. If had been recorded, it would have been impossible.

In addition, insurance and investment professionals feel more passion and excitement when they are inviting their prospects to listen to LIVE WEBINAR from an author who is going to unveil how to accumulate more money for retirement.

(Continued on next page)

7

You can triple your income by using some of these Prospecting Programs.

(Should the webinar be live or should it be recorded? continued)

On the other hand, a RECORDED CALL can be heard 24/7, there are no phone charges since the prospect can listen and watch your presentation on their computer screen, and there are vendors who specialize in recorded web conference presentations. Are there any disadvantages other than those discussed above? Yes, the audio quality of a recorded call is often average at best. Suggestion! Consider getting your recorded call done in an audio studio where the walls are padded, the microphone is high quality, and music can be added at the beginning, at the end and even when you are about to say something real important.

The cost for you to do a recorded call could be less than $200 for a 30 minute web conference. Can you spend more? We may have invested over $5,000 getting our *75 Secrets* book on audio since we have 3 narrators; Jane reading the Secret title, me giving the entire Secret, and Mike reading the disclaimer at the end of each secret plus we added 5 different "beds of music" and special sounds whenever we were introducing items in a series like the 5 best benefits or the 4 major reasons.

Webinar Tips

Have web conferences always been the most convenient, easiest, and problem-free way to present? No. They have been challenging."Boy, have they been challenging". However, we now know almost all of the pitfalls such as the following:

When selecting company(ies) for your web conferences, ask them if them if they can do the following:

Disable entry and exit sounds

1. Ask your conference vendor if they can disable all entry and exit sounds? Said differently, not too long ago, we gave a presentation and then I said, "Let's now listen to the host of this web conference, the one who made all of this possible today." We then heard 450 annoying exit sounds as 450 of the 500 attending began hanging up the phone during the next 10 seconds.

No roll call nor listing of names

2. You do not want a roll call. In other words, you do not want other attendees to hear or see the names of the attendees. Said differently, you do not want them to see that they are the only attendee, or that their neighbor or pastor is also considering a product. Privacy is an important issue.

Mute the audience

3. You want all participants muted or you want the power to mute the audience at the onset. I used to say that the most beautiful sound in the world is a baby's cry, meaning the birth of a baby; however, I have stopped saying that. Two months ago, a baby cried throughout our 30-minute presentation since the host of the conference did not know how to mute the audience. He now knows.

(Continued on next page)

7

You can triple your income by using some of these Prospecting Programs.

(Webinar Tips continued)

Recording

4. You want the ability to record for legal and or compliance reasons. A recording will also help you improve your presentation.

Reports

5. You need a report of who attended. This way you'll know the best people to contact after the consumer webinar.

The report also should show when they exited since the exit time could signal when you went too long or when the topic was less interesting.

Toll Free Number

6. There is a reason why every business in America has a toll free number. Clients and prospects want to call a toll free number. especially if the call is 15-30 minutes. If you are inviting consumers outside of your local area, use a toll free number.

How do you get people to attend?

There are many ways such as email invitations, postcards, letters, newsletters, and direct mail. Soon, we might experiment with voice messaging where 1 message will go out to thousands and thousands like the politicians do during election time. However, insurance and investment professionals and other professions are faced with a lot more "voice messaging" restrictions than the politicians. In addition, always tell your insurance company and or Broker Dealer what you are planning to do or say.

Since you need to use the economics of scale, email invitations may be the best way of reaching out to thousands of people. And, at the risk of repeating what we will say in Prospecing Approach #7 Email Campaigns, spend more time writing and testing the subject line(s) of your email. If no one opens your email, the 24 hours that you spent writing the copy in the body of the email is meaningless. They have to open your email first. More on that in the email part of this secret.

You come first. Content comes second.

No matter how great your content is, three things must be established in order for you to build your clientele with Consumer Webinars:

1. You need to build rapport and trust with the audience. As they're listening to you speak, you want them saying to their spouse, "My, isn't he a nice man".

2 You don't need to give the audience 30 different ideas; you only need to give them two or three, but make sure they are unforgettable ideas.

3. At every web conference, either you convince the audience that they need you or they convince you that you are not needed.

It is as simple as that.

7 *You can triple your income by using some of these Prospecting Programs.*

Questions & Answers Relating To Consumer Webinars

- Should you ask questions during your live consumer webinar? In our opinion, no.

- What is the ideal length of a consumer webinar? 15-20 minutes.

- Should there be a sign-in so you know who attends? Absolutely, yes.

- Should you be licensed in every state?

  Yes, if you are asking them to buy a product from you, unquestionably, you should be licensed in every state in which a person is listening.

- Should there be proper disclosure?

  Absolutely; speak to your insurance company, Broker/ Dealer about the words they want at the bottom of your web presentation and about the words you are planning to say.

The Beginning of New Dawn

We are at the beginning of a New Dawn that could change how products are presented and sold.

Soon, some marketing organizations and insurance companies will begin doing consumer webinars almost immediately after they hear what we are doing. Hopefully, they will select us to help them so we can do them every month of the year instead of just August.

If you have an insurance company or marketing organization in mind, tell us so we can email an online version of this section on Consumer Webinars to them.

Prospecting Approach #3:
The Most Overlooked Generation

Before we unveil who to call, let's examine why we need to call them. But, before we do, allow me to ask you a few questions first. For the most part, do you spend most of your prospecting time reaching out to people who are nearing retirement or to people who are already retired? When you call them, what % of the time do you get a voice message? 100%? What % of the time do they return your phone call? Never? And, how many other insurance and investment professionals are calling them? A zillion? Kind of difficult, isn't it?

So who should you begin calling and, more importantly, why should you call them? Beginning today, during non-productive time, we want you to begin calling people between the ages of 35 to 45. Why? Actually, there are 2 reasons why we want you to call them, one great reason and one very, very selfish reason.

#1 They need a professional more than anyone else. They need to be taught:

a) the importance of paying themselves first

b) to stay out of credit card debt

c) their fiscal responsibilities as a spouse and Dad and Mom

d) how to protect their mortgage with life insurance

e) how to keep their grocery bag full even during disability

f) how to calculate how much life insurance is enough

g) the power of employer matching with 401(k)s

h) how taxes and inflation can devour 100% of their taxable interest

i) the power of qualified retirement plans

j) the importance of owning a home

k) the value of term insurance at certain stages and the value of permanent life insurance

You can triple your income by using some of these Prospecting Programs.

l) the major advantages of redirecting money going to less important things like burger & fries, cigarettes, 32 oz. sodas, and Venti coffee to important things like life & health insurance premiums

m) a one time gift of $2,000 to a baby born today could be worth millions later

n) what a financial pyramid is and why their pyramid should be different than their parent's pyramid

o) the importance of having 5 professionals around their "Round Table"

p) the importance of thinking about their money on a regular basis

q) how to "Catch Tax Deferral"

So the first reason you should call them is that they need you badly since few insurance and investment professionals, if any, are calling them.

#2 But, before I unveil the second and very selfish reason to call them, allow me to tell you a "Secret". My daughter, Elizabeth, lives in Colorado. She has a great husband and two great unforgettable children. If my daughter called me and said the following words,

"Dad, we met a _____(CPA or attorney or etc.) and he really took great care of us. And, he would also take great care of you and Mom. You should meet with him."

Do you know the chances of me getting together with that professional the next time Mrs. H. and I are back in Colorado? About 100%.Friends, the best and easiest way to help 60 year old plus people is through their adult daughter or son. First of all, reach out to a younger clientele and give them a pleasant buying experience. Second, help their parents.

(Prospecting Approach #3: The Most Overlooked Generation continued)

How do you find the best 35-45 year olds to call? There are lead programs who can help you begin a drip program with 35-45 year olds or any age group in any section of the country. Reach out to these prospects. They need you.

As innovative as some lead programs are, W.V.H., Inc. still feels that the first appointment depends upon your phone skills and whether you have made a good first impression. And the conversion from a prospect to a client again depends upon you; you pinpointing the need, you showing the importance of solving that need now, and you building the rapport and trust with that soon-to-be-client.

With any lead program, start off small. Try it out first. Then ramp up after you experience success.

How do you reach out to these 35-45 year olds? Begin a "drip program". They get your letters, postcards, warm phone calls, newsletters, webinar invitations, warm phone calls, emails and warm phone calls.

Your next step? Call your 10 youngest clients and ask them if they would like you to help their parents like you have helped them. (make sure you are licensed in the state where the parent lives; if not, get licensed first)

You can triple your income by using some of these Prospecting Programs.

You
are
one
page
away
from

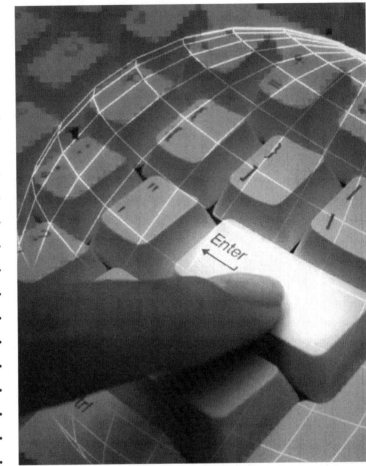

· · ·
·
·
·
·
·
·
·
·
·
·
·

· · · learning how your clients can help you get new clients.

Prospecting Approach #4:
Client Appreciation Events

Would you like to know a secret about the financial services industry? In spite of all the magazine articles, books, web conferences, and emails devoted to client seminars, less than 10% of all insurance and investment professionals will do a seminar over the next 12 months. That's right. In spite of seminars being one of the major reasons why many of the most successful professionals succeed, a shocking low percentage of professionals will turn to client seminars to reach the next level of success.

Why will so few do a client seminar during the next 12 months? Actually, there are four reasons. First of all, there are more people who fear speaking in public than fear flying. Second, the perception is that doing client seminars "cost" a lot of money. Third, they sense or have read that attendance is down. Fourth, they have already tried client seminars. While we are still bullish on Client Seminars as you read in Secret 5, we do feel that one of the easiest and least expensive ways to reach the next level of success is the Client Appreciation Event.

Before we unveil why Client Appreciation Events can take you to next level, let's define a Client Appreciation Event. A Client Appreciation Event is an opportunity for you to invite your clients to a venue like a picnic, minor league baseball game, restaurant, or an ice cream parlor where they are encouraged to bring along a friend, neighbor, or their adult son or daughter.

Why do Client Appreciation Events work so well?

#1 Your clients see how much your other clients like and respect you. More importantly, the guests of your clients also see the rapport and trust that you have with your clientele.

#2 You do not speak for 60-75 minutes like with a client seminar; you speak for only 5-15 minutes.

#3 Your investment can be 95% less than a client seminar. In other words, instead of investing $5,000, you can invest $250 or less.

#4 They are fun, informal, and relaxing.

You can triple your income by using some of these Prospecting Programs.

What are the Key Components of a Successful Client Appreciation Event?

#1 Do not spend more time with any one client. Welcome. Mingle. Shake hands. Smile when it is sincere.

#2 Try to remember the first names of most of your clients' guests. This can be done if you repeat their first name during the introduction and when you are about to move on to the next client. First name retention is also easier if you connect their name with something they are wearing or with a friend of yours that has the same name. At one time, I could remember the first names of at least 60-75 seminar attendees with only a handful of minor mistakes along the way. One major mistake was calling the Vice President of the company who hired me to speak the wrong first name 10 times. Now, his closest associates call him by the same wrong name. So, I guess, you can even have fun with the mistakes. Roll with the mistakes. Have fun. None of us are perfect but ALL of us can care about our clients more than ourselves.

#3 Do not discuss business. If a client wishes to discuss business, we suggest that you ask them if you could answer that question right after the event is over, either over the phone or at their place.

Your 5-15 Minute Presentation at the Client Appreciation Event

If you are an investment professional, consider giving the audience late breaking news, such as what the stock market did that day and your positive analysis on one segment of the economy, whether it be technology, global, or utilities.

If you are an insurance and/or an investment professional, consider giving:

• your "A" material. In other words, that short presentation that you've given over 1,000 times.

(Your 5-15 Minute Presentation at the Client Appreciation Event continued)

- or if your event is at an ice cream parlor, consider discussing the three flavors of saving money for retirement: taxable, tax-deferred, and tax-free (and be kind to CDs and Muni Bonds).

- or if your event is at a baseball game, consider discussing "Catching Tax-Deferral".

- or consider saying the following words during your Client Appreciation 5-15 minute presentation: "Friends, I just bought a $75 book that will help me help my clients" (hold the book up) "a book that unveils ways of accumulating more money for retirement by using proven concepts, forgotten strategies, and overlooked concepts. The secret that will help most of you at this event today is Secret #" (now say the Secret #, read the title of the Secret from your book, even read the short paragraph on the title page, and then either read or paraphrase the words that are on the following pages).

What are the best Secrets from our *75 Secrets* book for your Client Appreciation Event?

Secret #23 A one-time $2,000 gift to a baby born today could be worth $1 million dollars.

Secret #25 The IRS allows people 50 and older to catch up and contribute an extra $5,500 to their 401(k).

Secret #31 Surround yourself with 5 mentors and be like Warren, JFK, and King Arthur.

Secret #34 Think about your money on a quarterly basis.

Secret #38 Figure out, without a pen or calculator, how many years it will take for your money to double.

(Continued on next page)

You can triple your income by using some of these Prospecting Programs.

(What are the best Secrets from our 75 Secrets book for your Client Appreciation Event continued)

Secret #40 There is an easy way to compute what your advisors are worth to you.

Secret #43 How my Uncle Donald started with one penny and became filthy rich. (tell it with a smile on your face)

Secret #51 You could be losing 30% of your bank interest every year, maybe more. (use a dollar bill for a prop)

Secret #53 You can reduce the income taxes you are paying on your Social Security income.

Secret #55 A non-qualified annuity's tax advantages are overlooked by most IRA owners.

48 hours after the event

Within 48 Hours following the Appreciation Event, call all clients, thank them for attending and schedule an annual review. Following the annual review, use the referral approach that we discussed in Secret 4 by taking out your referral folder, getting the full name, occupation, phone number, etc. of the guest that they invited to the Client Appreciation Event, and their OK to call them.

The purposes of a Client Appreciation Event are:

1) to show your clients that you appreciate them being part of your clientele

2) schedule annual reviews

3) to meet new prospects, in other words, your clients' friends, neighbors, and the adult children whom they invited to your event.

Prospecting Approach #5: The Names of the Most Overlooked People Are in Your File Cabinet

Have you ever started your day off by saying you had no one to call that day? Have you ever purchased leads or considered purchasing leads because you had no one to call? Do you think that your income would increase if you only had more people to call? If you answered "Yes" to any of those questions, we have a great "Secret" to share with you. What is that "Secret"? You not only have plenty of people to call but you also have the best people to call.

Please think of your file cabinet(s). You have every application for every current client and former client. You probably even have every illustration or proposal you ever presented to a prospect.

Friends, you have a GOLD MINE OF LEADS. "Health insurance clients" who are "Leads" for annuities or life insurance or vise versa. "Former Clients" who are "Leads" since they need to hear your voice and see your face soon. "Current prospects" who are still "Leads" since you have to show them that they have a need and the best time to solve that need is now.

Step 1
Over the next 2 days, call the following

Day 1. Call 5 current prospects who probably did not buy an annuity from you because of the surrender charges and use the new ways to discuss surrender charges in Secret 9.

Day 2. Call 5 people you know that have money in the bank and use the words and questionnaire on pages 236 and 237.
(Continued on next page)

7

You can triple your income by using some of these Prospecting Programs.

(Prospecting Approach #5: The Names of the Most Overlooked People Are in Your File Cabinet continued)

Step 2
Hire a high school or college student and ask them to go to your file cabinet and create an Excel sheet with the following categories:

1) names of all of your clients, former clients, and current prospects

2) the type they are such as clients, former clients and current prospects

3) their date of birth

4) their occupation and industry like doctor/medicine and

5) the date of the first application that you ever completed for that client; just the first application, or your first date of contact

Step 3
Go to the last section in this book and read The Next 30 Days but only one day at a time. If you do, you will have 25 extra people to call every week. And, if you like to "double-size ", you will have 50 extra people to call every week.

But, first re-read our Secret 2, *Using The Phone*. Second, call. Third, meet and help more people since they need you. Four, move to the product and concept that ignites your passion.

Prospecting Approach #6: Hallmark Birthday Cards

Are you ready for a real oldie? A cool oldie? A forgotten approach for so many of us? A tip that will get you to rock and roll all the way to the bank with commission checks in both back pockets? More importantly, are you ready to show your clients that you care?

I have been in the financial services industry since 1975 and I have met a lot of great people. At one time, someone calculated that well over 200,000 insurance and investment professionals have attended our seminars. And heaven only knows how many have attended our live web conferences. One client of ours gets almost 1,000 insurance and investment professionals to listen every month. And that is just one of our clients.

Take a guess to how many people in the business world send me a birthday card every year. 500? 1000? 2,000? Every year, I get only 2 birthday cards, one from Bob, the gentleman who bought my agency in 1983, and one from Neil, my State Farm agent for the past 27 years. Only 2! But, the funny thing is that every year–near my birthday–I think of Bob and Neil for a few seconds and wonder if they are going to send me another birthday card.

Friends, how many clients think of you on their birthday? Suggestion: Be part of your client's birthday. At the least, send them a Hallmark birthday card. At the most, send their kids one too. Remember this is a relationship business.

Why Hallmark? I have a dear friend, Mr. Anderson, whose spouse works for Hallmark. Mr. Anderson says that Hallmark is a great company and they have a great retirement plan for their employees. In my opinion, the more birthday cards you buy, the more comfortable my friend's retirement will be.
(Continued on next page)

7

You can triple your income by using some of these Prospecting Programs.

Can you do something slightly more than send them a birthday card?

Yes, you can. In 2009, I called all of my clients on their birthday and left a short message by singing the four words "Happy Birthday To You" followed by "This is Bill Harris, happy birthday." I never added anything about business. It was a personal phone call.

One day, one of my clients, Heath, called back. While he called to talk about business, the first thing he said was "Bill, you were the 2nd person to sing "Happy Birthday to me today" and then he began talking about business. During the entire telephone call, I kept on thinking about the other person who had sung to Heath that morning. When he was done talking business, he said

"Bill, thanks for the phone call this morning. My Mom called earlier and she too sang "Happy Birthday" to me." I quickly replied without even thinking, "Heath, that is nice company for me to be in."

Friends, have any of your clients put you into a category with their Mom or Dad even for just 1 second. At the least, send a birthday card but why not give them a call and sing the four words "Happy Birthday To You." It is easy when you really really like the person you are calling.

Prospecting Approach #7: Email Campaigns

I know how many emails you get every day. Heck, we get a zillion too. While the consumer gets a lot too, surprisingly, the consumer is not getting many emails about insurance-related products. While that will change, now could be the best time to put into action a series of email campaigns. First of all, what is an email campaign? We define an "email campaign" as your new way to reach out to a "specific audience" in order "for you to get what you want".

The "email campaign" can be:

- small and as primitive as just you and current email program or

- just you and a email service such as Constant Contact, Jango Mail, or Campaigner; the latter one being the one we currently use or

- you, an email service, and "an email specialist", our "email specialist" is Josh

The "email campaign" could involve:

- one email every week over a period of time like 6 months or a year

- emails with "a look" consistent with your letterhead or web site or both

- an email that clearly tells the benefits to the email recipient if they:

  - ask for a brochure or

  - register for a wcb conference or

  - schedule an appointment or

  - just ask for more informative emails from you

You can triple your income by using some of these Prospecting Programs.

The "Specific Audience" that gets your emails can be all or some of the following:

- your current prospects

- your former clients

- your clients

Please note that in the 3 above examples, the people who are getting your emails ALL know you.

Get What You Want

Getting what you want can be as simple as:

increasing the number of annuity clients or

doubling the number of health insurance accounts or

selling more books

What are the 2 advantages to using email campaigns as a way to build your clientele?

#1 Cost

The cost of an email campaign can be dramatically less than many other prospecting programs. For example, our email database is around 12,500 email addresses and we pay our email service, Campaigner, around $70 a month for an easy way to build emails, send emails, and, more importantly, to save and track email results.

Our email specialist, Josh, while bright, caring, and helpful is also affordable. Just yesterday, we received an invoice for $300 from him for creating 6 similar but different emails and getting them inside our Campaigner accounts so they launch at six different times.

(Continued on next page)

(2 advantages of using email campaigns continued)

#2 Convenience

With many other prospecting programs, you have to be there "in suit and tie". With emailing, you can remain in your pajamas or stay in the gym.

What are the disadvantages?

Unless you are unusually gifted, bright or lucky, it will take you time before you figure out the best email look, the best subject lines for your emails, best offers, best copy, and best times to send the email. However, if you have patience and if you like to test subject lines and study results, "an email campaign" should be "one" of the ways you build your clientele.

Did I just say that "an email campaign" should be the "only" way you build your clientele or did I just say that "an email campaign" should be "one" of the ways you build your clientele. Yes, you want it to be one of the ways.

Very Important Do's and Don'ts

1. Show your email to your insurance company(ies), Broker-Dealer, etc before sending it out

2. Have your name, mailing address, and telephone number on the email

3. Only reach out to consumers who live in a state where you have an insurance license

4. Allow them to unsubscribe and take them off your list immediately if they unsubscribe *(Continued on next page)*

You can triple your income by using some of these Prospecting Programs.

(Important do's and don'ts continued)

5. Check and re-check your spelling and grammar

6. Spend more time writing and testing the
    subject lines of the email than the time you spend
    writing the body of the email

Think about it. You spend hours and hours writing and rewriting the body of the email and then 60 seconds or less on the subject line.

> "Friends, if your email does not have an enticing subject line, they will not open it. And, if they do not open your email, they will not see what you have to offer."

Step 1. Always create 2 subject lines. Get 20% of your email database and send half of them one subject line and the other half the other subject line. And, when you select that 20%, make sure they are the same type like "all clients" or"all current prospects". Two weeks ago, we sent the same email with the same subject line to our "clients' and "prospective clients". The open rate was 400% greater with our clients. So when testing the subject lines, test 2 groups that are almost identical. On the other hand, if you wanted to test which group was better, like those who attended your seminar or those who get your newsletter, then you would keep everything identical since you are testing for the better list.

Step 2. Go to your email service's web site, login, and look at the results of your email. Look at the open rate percentage, in other words, what % of them opened your email. Look at the "click on" percentage, in other words, what % of them clicked on something that was in the body of your email like your offer, or to register, or your web site.

These are just 2 examples to how you can tweak, refine, and almost master the best way to make the best offer.

(Continued on next page)

(Important do's and don'ts continued)

7. Email on the best day at the best time

Quick question from me to you. When you arrived at your computer this morning, how many emails were waiting there for you to read—including those suspected as spam? For me, since I just counted, it was 110 emails suspected as spam and 10 emails suspected as "legit". So in other words, whomever sends me an email after I went to bed and before I arrived at my computer is competing with 119 other emails for my attention. However, whoever sends me an email at 11:00 A.M. today, will get almost all of my attention.

Next Step. Try to learn the best times and best days to send your emails. While we can tell you the best times and best days to send emails to insurance and investment professionals, it appears that the best times and best days to send emails to your clients and prospects will be different.

And the best days and times can change. For example, 7 months ago, we were elated when we discovered that an invite we sent on Saturday broke all records for us. Sadly, because it is now summer or because others discovered that Saturday was sales-creating, recent Saturday's have been disappointing. Will we return to Saturday? Absolutely! Please remember to test and sample.

You can triple your income by using some of these Prospecting Programs.

Speaking of remembering, please remember,

"An email campaign should not be the "only" way you build your clientele. However, it be should be "one" of the ways you build your clientele.

When you combine the low cost and convenience of an email campaign with the common sense approach of telling your story to thousands at the same time with an email, you can increase your clientele."

Things to Remember

1. Your email should clearly tell the email recipient the benefits if they respond.

2. Cost and convenience are 2 major advantages.

3. You must have patience and the willingness to test and study results.

4. Your subject line controls how many open your email.

5. Show your insurance companies and Broker Dealer what you are planning to email.

6. Be licensed in the state where the email recipients live.

Prospecting Approach #8: Direct Mail

In my opinion, there are two types of mailers. The first kind would be the mass mailer (1,000 or more). You mail and wait for the post card like replies to be mailed back to you. Not too long ago, a 6% response rate was possible. Soon we will reach out to an industry expert and find out how much that 6% has plummeted. Naturally, the success of this campaign depends upon the mass mailer vendor you select, the names that you or they selected, and how proficient you are at scheduling appointments, presenting, overcoming objections, and closing. If you read this entire book, you should be in great shape.

The second type of mailer is one in which "you"" mail 25-50 letters and call everyone. In this instance, the success of this campaign depends upon just "you" and the names that you selected. Arguably, your phone skills are slightly more important with this type of mailer since you still need to create the interest. With the mass mailer, the post card like replies are those who are interested.

Which one is better for you?

Your budget, your phone skills for creating the interest, testimonials from colleagues of yours who have had success with a vendor should point you in the right direction.

As you have heard before, every "no" brings you closer to a "yes." We just have to ask. We are in the asking profession. A profession that has no ceiling on what we can make and how many people we can help. A profession that allows us to give clients more money later and more income later. A profession that can change the retirement lifestyle of millions of people across America. The profession of helping people protect the people that they love. The profession of selling insurance products.

You can triple your income by using some of these Prospecting Programs.

**You
are
one
page
away
from**

. . . learning about a FREE way to get new clients.

secret **7**

Prospecting Approach #9: Radio Show Interview

Radio is good business. In fact, anything that is free, gives you exposure, and gives thousands of consumers the opportunity of saying "yes" to you is smart business.

Free? Just call the program director of any financial show. They have many hours of programming time to fill. When you call, be brief and professional. You should refer to some of the household name magazines that have done stories recently on retirement. Remind the program director to that their listeners will benefit. Have a good hook! In our instance, we would use any of the 75 Secrets in our book as a hook such as

> Secret #53 You can reduce or eliminate the income taxes that you are paying unnecessarily on Social Security income.

Since so many of you already own our *75 Secrets* book already, send us an email asking for our written OK to use any of *75 Secrets* on radio. Our top radio Secrets are on page 204 & 205.

When talking to the program director, you should do a strong and brief commercial on yourself. In essence, tell the program director why you are special and different. As a result of this conversation, many of you will succeed and get on radio shows for free. Toward the end of your conversation with the program director, ask for their permission so you can play the radio show interview on your website. Good exposure for them. Career enhancing for you. *(Continued on next page)*

7

You can triple your income by using some of these Prospecting Programs.

(Prospecting Approach #9: Radio Interview continued)

Before you go on radio, you should send an email and letter to all of your clients, former clients, current prospects and every successful person you want as your client. Tell them about the radio show interview. Tell them the topic, what they will learn, benefits of them listening, your telephone number. Tell them everything but the station name and what time it airs. If these prospects are interested, they will feel comfortable calling and asking you for the station and the time of the show. You will now know which prospects to call after the show, won't you?

15 days after the radio show interview, invite all of your clients, former clients, current prospects and every successful person you want as your client to your website to listen to your pass code protected radio show interview. Tell them what they will learn if they do listen. Tell them the password. Why a password? You want to know who has listened to your radio show interview on your web site.

Get
the
radio
show's
program
director

-
-
-
-
-
-
-
-
-
-
-
-
-
- . . . to invite you back by giving the listening audience some of the great content on the following 2 pages.

7

You can triple your income by using some of these Prospecting Programs.

THE BEST SECRETS FOR A RADIO SHOW INTERVIEW (please remember to ask for our written permission first to discuss any of these on radio)

Secret	Secret Title
1.	You can have more than one million dollars FDIC insured at one bank.
2.	FDIC reports that almost 20% of all bank deposits are not insured.
3.	Laddering CDs gives you liquidity plus protects you from interest rate volatility.
4.	CD interest rates are far more volatile than you think.
6.	Taxes and inflation can devour all of your interest.
11.	The Social Security system will probably change.
12.	It might be smarter for some to get the smaller Social Security benefit at age 62.
14.	Converting your IRA to a ROTH IRA could be a big mistake or the best thing you ever do.
19.	What you do in the first five years of retirement controls if you go broke or leave a legacy.
21.	Excess withdrawals from a retirement account is the #1 reason why retirees go broke.
30.	Review the Social Security Statement that you get every year with your professionals.

THE BEST SECRETS FOR A RADIO SHOW INTERVIEW
(please remember to ask for our written permission first to discuss any of these on radio)

Secret   Secret Title

31. Surround yourself with five mentors and be like Warren, JFK, and King Arthur.

34. Think about your money on a quarterly basis.

38. Figure out without a pen or calculator how many years it will take for your money to double.

45. There are 5 risks potentially more devastating than risk to principal.

53. You can reduce the income taxes that you are paying on your Social Security income.

55. A non-qualified annuity's tax advantages are overlooked by most IRA owners.

57. You can now get tax deferral and monthly income at the same time.

62. Who you designate as annuitant and beneficiary can be a costly mistake.

70. Smart people select insurance companies to insure everything important to them.

72. 97% of all Indexed Annuities credit interest based on one index but that might change.

You can triple your income by using some of these Prospecting Programs.

You are one page away from

. . . using the advice given to me from a very seasoned TV producer.

Prospecting Approach #10: Television

If giving 25 to 50 seminar attendees an opportunity to buy in one hour is smart business, what would you call giving 250,000 prospects an opportunity to buy in 5 minutes? We call it TV.

Eight ways to receive maximum results on TV(local ABC, NBC, CBS, FOX affiliate)

1. The easiest way to get on TV is to write a book. Your book does not have to be a top-seller. Your book does not have to be in every bookstore in America. You just have to be an author, the book needs a catchy title, and the book must have at least 2-4 very, very interesting proven approaches, overlooked concepts, or forgotten strategies about accumulating money.

2. Send a letter to all of the TV producers in your local area. Your letter should capture the essence of your book and how their audience would benefit. TV producers love local authors.

3. When the TV producer expresses interest in you, ask the TV producer for permission for you to play the TV interview on your website after the interview. Great exposure for the station. And, as you will soon find out, prospecting-generating and sales-creating for you.

4. After the TV station confirms that you will appear on TV, tell all of your clients, former clients, current prospects via email and letter that you will appear. Tell them the station and approximate time. Also, send a letter to every successful executive and business owner in your area whom you would like to be your next client.

5. The TV Interview: Give the interviewer your biography and the questions he or she should ask. If they ask you the wrong question, use a transitional word or phrase and answer the question you want to answer. You can control the order of information that you give, not the interviewer.

(Continued on next page)

(Prospecting Approach #10 continued)

6. Naturally, you will have your book with you. However, your mission is not to sell your book. Your mission is to enhance your image in your community and increase your clientele by adding some of the most successful executives and business owners to your clientele.

7. After the TV interview, send an email and letter to all of your clients, former clients, current prospects and every successful executive and business owner in your area whom you would like to be your next client. Tell them how much you enjoyed the TV interview and that you would like to stop by to show them a proven approach from the book; plus give them a FREE copy of your book.

8. Put the TV interview up on your website and send an additional email and letter to the same parties inviting them to your website 15 days later.

Ways to receive maximum results on much smaller TV stations

Not too long ago, we were a frequent guest on TV for a very small TV station in Los Angeles. However, our "TV career" could have stopped after the first show. After the first show, one of the veteran producers pulled me aside and said,

"I bet you do a great seminar but you are doing a lousy job on TV. Bill, your stories are too long for TV. You have to shorten everything. More importantly, you have to show your audience what you will send them if they call-in. Wave it in the air. Show them what they can get."

My next TV appearance was the following month. In fact, it was on St. Patrick's Day at 6:00 A.M. I waved. I was concise. I was excited. The results? We broke that TV's station record for the number of call-ins.

In summary, giving 250,000 people the opportunity to know, like, and respect you in 5 minutes is "The TV Business".

8

You can have even more phone success by using these phone scripts.

A s you are aware, the words we use are as important to us as a calm hand is to a surgeon. And, they are even more important when we use the phone since your voice and words are everything. On the following pages, you will get 2 time tested phone scripts. The first one is terrific since it is needs-based and it is designed for every name in your file cabinet. The second script is out of this world for cold-calling since it allows you to use the words FREE and complimentary. The other 8 scripts represent the 8 topics that most professionals and consumers are most passionate about. You are 1 page away from more phone success.

8 *You can have even more phone success by using these phone scripts.*

Proven Phone Scripts

1. Inflation-fighting Birthday Script

Your file cabinet is a gold mine of almost everyone's date of birth. Today, call 10 clients, former clients, and current prospects who were born in 1960 and say,

In 1960, the year you were born, a newspaper cost 6¢, a brand new car cost $1,627, and a home in some sections of the United States cost $11,900.

Question #1: "Do you think that a newspaper, car, and home will cost more 10 years from now than they do today?

Question #2: "What are you doing about this problem? "And, after they say "Nothing" or just shrug their shoulders, ask

Question #3: "Would you like me to show you how to potentially lessen the impact that inflation can have on your retirement dollars?"

Tomorrow and everyday thereafter, call 10 more clients, former clients and current prospects using what things cost the year they were born.

Where do you find what things cost? Google it or revisit pages 348-349 in our *75 Secrets* book since it has what things cost for every year from 1936 to 1985.

Free and complimentary script for any cold call

"Hello, my name is _____ and I have been an insurance professional in this community for ___ years. The reason why I am calling is that I would like to stop by and give you a FREE gift certificate from your favorite coffee shop and a complimentary review of your insurance and retirement program. (sincere smile in voice) Where is the best place for us to get together? Your place, my place or at your favorite coffee shop?

Will they say, "Yes come on over now!"? No, there will be indecision. There will be silence or you will hear an objection. Regardless, say," I can appreciate how you feel but 3 things can happen when we get together and you win all 3 ways. You either find out that everything is perfect or you'll find out that you have too much insurance or not enough. (sincere smile in voice) Where is the best place for us to get together? Your place, my place or at your favorite coffee shop near by?

8 *You can have even more phone success by using these phone scripts.*

Since we have such a loyal clientele, it is very common for our clients to own all of our books. With that in mind, here are 8 more phone scripts. These scripts work remarkably well if you select the Secret that ignites your passion. Needless to say, the words "It is a $75 book that helps me help my clients" are priceless.

Phone Scripts

1. Phone call to almost everyone receiving Social Security

"I just bought a book titled *75 Secrets: An Insider's Guide to Bank CDs, Annuities and Retirement Planning*. It's a $75 book that helps me help my clients. On page 212, there is a form that takes only 3 minutes to complete. And you know something, you might be paying income taxes unnecessarily on your Social Security Income. Where is the best place for us to get together since we might be able to give you a pay raise? Your place, my place or at a coffee shop nearby.

2. Phone call to almost everyone who owns CDs

I just bought a book titled *75 Secrets: An Insider's Guide to Bank CDs, Annuities and Retirement Planning*. It's a $75 book that helps me help my clients. On page 15, there is a chart from the Federal Reserve that surprisingly shows the interest rate volatility of CDs. You have to see this chart. Where is the best place for us to get together since I know you do not like sharp decreases in your interest rates. Your place, my place or at a coffee shop nearby

3. Phone call to almost everyone who has a passbook savings, money market accounts and CDs

"I just bought a book titled *75 Secrets: An Insider's Guide to Bank CDs, Annuities and Retirement Planning*. It's a $75 book that helps me help my clients. On page 346-347, it shows the tax bracket and inflation for every year from 1936-1980. And, when you study this chart as I have, it shows that most of the time taxes and inflation devour all of the interest. You really should see this chart. Where is the best place for us to get together so you can begin getting a higher return? Your place, my place or at a coffee shop nearby.

4. Phone call to anyone who needs life or health insurance but cannot afford the premium.

"I just read a book that unveils how simple it is to afford insurance by simply redirecting some of the money they spend everyday on (say either coffee, cigarettes, or a 48 ounce soda) to an insurance premium that has a lot more value than (say with a smile in your voice " a cup of joe", "a cig" or "way too much cola") Where is the best place for us to get together since you can now get the insurance you said you wanted but could not afford? Best place to meet? How about your place?(if no quick response) What about Starbucks near work?"

5. Phone call to anyone you know who may have lost 40% of their money in 2008-2009

"I just read a book that reinforces 2 things we both know. #1 No one has a crystal ball to where the stock market will be going. Maybe up? Maybe down? #2 The most prudent thing to do is to reposition some of your money to products that (say either "cannot go down 40%" or "have a guaranteed selling price every year"). Where is the best place for us to get together so we can look at some prudent alternatives? Your place, my place or at a coffee shop nearby."

6. Phone call to any small business owner.

"Joe, this is Bill Harris, an insurance professional in this city for 30 years, I would like to stop by, shake hands with you, and show you the IRS brochure 5305 SEP that allows small business owners like yourself to slash their income taxes by opening a Simplified Pension Plan with a bank, insurance company, or mutual fund company. (smile in voice) Best time to stop by with coffee and donuts?"

7. Phone call to any grandparent or soon-to-be grandparent you know whose adult child is about to have a baby.

(using your passion) "Mary, you are one of the first 5 people I thought of this morning who would be most interested in helping your new grandchild (say either "become a millionaire" or "go to college" or "have the BIGGEST wedding in town some day. *(Continued on next page)*

8 *You can have even more phone success by using these phone scripts.*

(Phone call to any grandparent or soon-to-be grandparent continued)

All you need is $2,000 and the right product. Where is the best place for us to get together so your grandchild will always remember you? Your place, my place or at a coffee shop nearby."

8. Phone call to anyone 50 and older who is more apt to own 401(k).

"Herb, this is Bill Harris. One of the best kept secrets is that the IRS will allow YOU to "catch-up" and save more money in your 401(k) than someone age 49 and younger. Where is the best place for us to get together since this is the best way for you to reduce current taxes and accumulate more money for retirement. Best place to meet? What about at work? (if no quick response) Quick lunch at Joe's Diner?"

Bonus: We promised you 8 phone scripts. Here are 2 more. Friends, when possible, under promise and over deliver. Sometimes it is very easy to do.

9. Phone call to any former client.

"Max, this is a name from the past, Bill Harris. May I have 14 seconds of your time? Since we are only as strong as the people and advisors that surround us, I would like you to add me to your circle of mentors who offer you advice and opinions. I do not want to replace anyone but I do want to be added, especially now,since I have learned so much in the last (say the year when they became a former client)" Where is the best place for us to get together so you can begin getting a 2nd opinion? Best place to meet? Your place or your favorite coffee shop?"

10. Anyone who owns an IRA.

This is Bill Harris, an investment professional in this community for 35 years. There is a retirement annuity that can get pick up where your IRA leaves off. Your contribution can be much larger so you can potentially accumulate more money for retirement PLUS you do NOT have to begin taking withdrawals at 70.5. Where is the best place for us to get together so you can take advantage of current tax law? Best place to meet? Your place for 15 minutes or at your favorite coffee shop?"

secret 9

You can overcome any objection about surrender charges if you use this material.

Not too long ago, 300 insurance professionals used our "surrender charge" material and they wrote over 1.3 billion dollars of annuity and life premium. Because of this material, so many of us are going to be able to achieve a much higher level of selling success. Because of this material, annuity and life insurance presenting will be so much easier. And, far more importantly, because of this material, insurance and investment professionals will continue helping the general public retire with financial and emotional independence by providing full disclosure and a balanced and fair presentation.

9

You can overcome any objection about surrender charges if you use this material.

Naturally, insurance and investment professionals should ask their insurance companies for the way that their insurance companies want their surrender charges explained.

#1 Surrender Charges: Why Do Surrender Charges Exist: Run On The Bank

Isn't a surrender charge period an insurance company's way of attempting to protect itself from a run on the bank? Where do we want some of our retirement money? To be with an insurance company that is trying to protect itself from a run on the bank? Or, do we want some of our retirement money to be with an insurance company that is not trying to protect itself from a run on the bank?

A run on the bank. In order for an insurance company to provide a guaranteed interest rate for the life of the annuity or a competitive guaranteed interest rate for 1-10 years, the insurance company needs to purchase obligations like government and corporate bonds. However, when interest rates rise, the value of a bond goes down in value prior to the bond's maturity.

So imagine a hypothetical annuity without SURRENDER CHARGES paying a 5% interest rate. What would those annuity contract holders of that hypothetical annuity do in renewal years if other annuities were paying 10% interest and they were still getting 5%? The annuity contract holders would "surrender." In other words, "cash in" their annuity or exchange their annuity for another annuity paying that 10% interest rate. In other words, there would be a run on the bank since there would be no surrender penalties holding them back from surrendering or exchanging their annuity.

And, wouldn't those annuity contract holders expect to get 100% of their premium and 100% of their interest since our hypothetical annuity did not have a surrender charge period? However, it would be more difficult for the insurer to give 100% of the premium and earnings to many of their contract holders if some of the bonds supporting the insurance company guarantees were selling for 75 cents on the dollar. And, some of the bonds could be selling at 75 cents on a dollar in an increasing interest rate environment.

That is why we say,

"Where do we want some of our retirement money? Do we want some of our retirement money to be with an insurance company that is trying to protect itself from a run on the bank? Or, do we want some of our retirement money to be with an insurance company that is not trying to protect itself from a run on the bank?" There must be three winners. The insurance company must win. And, above all, our clients must win. And, if they win, we can win!!!"

#2 Surrender Charges: Why Do Surrender Charges Exist: Compensation To Insurance Professionals

Since The Employee Benefit Research Institute reported that 50% of working Americans have $50,000 or less saved and 25% of them have 0% saved, the consumer needs an insurance professional now more than ever before. Surrender charges allow an insurance company to pay competitive commissions to an insurance and investment professional.

How do we define an insurance and investment professional? There are several ways, and here are a few. Some sales people —not professionals—measure success by how much money they made that day. Too often that short-sightedness delivers too many one year relationships with clients and too few referrals. On the other hand, professionals measure success in decades, so while "a lost sale" is still disappointing, "a lost sale" due to providing full disclosure is part of building a successful career.

In addition, professionals listen more than talk, care about the consumer more than themselves, tell a story of diversification, remain balanced and fair by sharing the advantages and disadvantages of each product and rider, and, above all, they are proud that the surrender charges are the 2nd best thing about presenting and owning an annuity.

9 *You can overcome any objection about surrender charges if you use this material.*

#3 Surrender Charges: Your Annuity Contract

What do you say if a prospect asks you, "What if I need to cash in my annuity because of an emergency?"

First of all, we shouldn't wait for the prospect to ask us about emergencies and surrender penalties. We should discuss surrender charges regardless of whether they ask or not. But, one proven approach of describing surrender charges is to show your actual annuity contract. More specifically, the pages in your annuity contract that deals with surrender charges.

Because once you show your annuity contract, all of a sudden, the client and/or prospect realizes that you too are concerned about retirement, that you wanted all of the following benefits, too: tax-deferred accumulation, potentially more money later, possible lifetime income, probate advantages later, insurance company penalty free access to 10% of your premium and earnings during the surrender charge period, insurance company penalty free access to 100% of your premium and earnings after the surrender charge period, all while your premium and earnings can be backed by the financial stability and claims paying ability of the insurance company issuing the annuity.

This "using your own annuity contract at the point-of-sale idea" can also be a great way to test and challenge your own objectivity especially if you own an annuity with a 5 year surrender charge period and you're presenting an annuity with a 45 year surrender charge period (exaggeration intended). If you don't own an annuity or if the annuity you own is different from the one that you're recommending, we recommend using a specimen annuity contract for the annuity that you're recommending with a legal pad where you're going to be able to show them examples of total surrender and excess withdrawals.

#4 Surrender Charges: Every Product Has A Penalty

What if you don't want to use the annuity contract at the point-of-sale? Then, you give another direct, clear explanation. "Mr. Jones, if you surrender this annuity during the surrender charge period, there will be surrender charges. If you surrender during the first year, there will be a 7% surrender charge, the following year 6% and then, 5%, 4%, 3%, 2%, 1%. And then, decreasing to 0% in year eight." So, assuming a $10,000 premium and assuming that your emergency were to occur during that first year, there would be a surrender charge of slightly over $700. In other words, 7%, the surrender charge penalty in the first year times $10,500, the premium plus earnings, resulting in a surrender penalty of $735.

Mr. Jones, doesn't almost every financial product have a surrender penalty of some kind? With Certificates of Deposit, we have penalties for premature surrender. In other words, loss of interest. With your home residence, the potential penalties would be the housing market when you sell the house. Not too long ago, you said to me, that you had $1 million dollars in taxable alternatives such as money market accounts, passbook savings, and Certificates of Deposit. And that you were considering putting $100,000 in this annuity. However, if an emergency were to arise, wouldn't you first go to your money market account and get some money there? And then, if you needed more money, to your passbook savings? And then, to your CD? And then, because of the annuity that I am recommending, you can withdrawal 10% of your annuity value each and every year, wouldn't you then go to your annuity?

What emergency in America could arise where you need $1 million dollars in one day?

9 *You can overcome any objection about surrender charges if you use this material.*

#5 Surrender Charges: Diversification

Objections about surrender charges often arise when we are putting too much of their money into any one financial product. Let me give you an example. Better yet, let me ask a question to everyone. Has a client ever told you that they had $100,000 in a Certificate of Deposit and it was maturing the following week? Did you ever go after "all" of that money?

And, did you ever drive home with none of that money? We should tell a story of diversification for two reasons, for a selfish reason and for an unselfish reason. The selfish reason is when you're going after their all, do you think that you are making it very, very easy for them to say yes to you? Or, are you increasing their anxiety level? So, reason number one we tell a story of diversification is for a selfish reason because we must learn and master how to make it very, very easy for people to say yes to us.

But, there is another reason why we should tell a story of diversification, a far more important reason, and that is no one should put a great deal of their dollars into any one given product, including an annuity.

#6 Surrender Charges: The Cost For Liquidity Is Reflected In The Interest Rate

Are there other ways to discuss surrender charges? Yes, but we must be direct and clear first. And then, use comparisons to show that surrender charges make all the sense in the world.

With many financial products, the cost for penalty free total access is often reflected in the interest rate credited. For example, saving money (smile in voice) under the mattress provides penalty free access to 100% of your money morning, afternoon, and night. But, the interest rate is only 0%. If you wake up at 3:00 in the morning and you want penalty free access to 100% of your money, no problem. Just reach down under the mattress and it's there, hopefully. (Smile)

However, if you want an interest rate higher than 0%, such as 1%, a far more reasonable alternative would be a money market account or passbook savings account where you get penalty free access to 100% of your money by visiting the bank or ATM.

If you want an interest rate higher than 1%, an alternative could be a Certificate of Deposit where penalty free access to 100% of your principal and interest is available at maturity such as in three months or in one year. Have you noticed that the interest rate has been higher each time penalty free access was restricted?

And, that logic of a potentially higher return continues with the annuity since fixed annuities can offer insurance company penalty free access to 10% of your premium and earnings during the surrender charge period and insurance company penalty free access to 100% of your premium and earnings after the surrender charge period of 5 or 10 years or more.

Doesn't it make sense for your clients to diversify so that they can have penalty free access to most of the money that they have in the bank while some of their money is accumulating on a tax–deferred basis with an annuity? Makes sense, doesn't it?

You can overcome any objection about surrender charges if you use this material.

#7 Surrender Charges: The Power of Disappearing Surrender Charges

The chart on the opposite page assumes a $10,000 premium growing at 5% with a hypothetical annuity that has a 10 year surrender charge period, a 10% surrender charge in year 1 declining 1% each year until it is 0% in year 11, and insurance company penalty-free access to 10% of the annuity value each year during the surrender charge period, and insurance company penalty-free access to 100% of the annuity value after the surrender charge period.

As you can see, the annuity can be a helpful retirement solution if you have set aside other dollars for things that might occur during the surrender charge period.

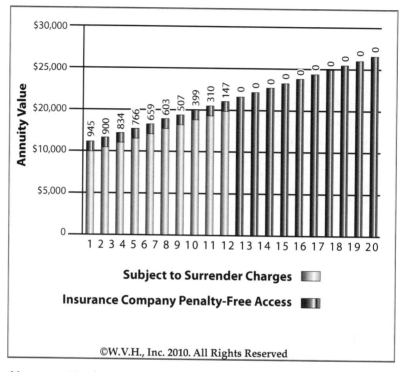

Annuity Value

$30,000

$25,000

$20,000

$10,000

$5,000

0

945 900 834 766 659 603 507 399 310 147

1 2 3 4 5 6 7 8 9 10 11 12 13 14 15 16 17 18 19 20

Subject to Surrender Charges

Insurance Company Penalty-Free Access

Most annuities have a surrender charge period of 5, 10 or more years. Annuities are not insured by the FDIC or any other agency and are subject to investment risks, including the possible loss of principal, Annuities have earnings which are taxable upon withdrawal, and if taken before age 59½, may be subject to a 10% Federal withdrawal penalty.

9

You can overcome any objection about surrender charges if you use this material.

#8 Surrender Charges: Worst Case Scenario

We think that many of you might be shocked to learn that "our worse case scenario", a surrender during the surrender charge period, can be appreciably better than the "worse case scenarios" for so many other products. On the following page, we show you one example.

However, in spite of that, the consumer should always have money set aside in passbook savings, money market accounts, and Certificates of Deposit for unexpected emergencies and be informed by you that surrender charges exist, how they work, and the actual penalty based on their annuity premium, surrender charge, and market value adjustment, if any. Why? An informed client is often the best client to have.

HYPOTHETICAL FIXED ANNUITY VALUE at 5%	SURRENDER CHARGE	CASH SURRENDER VALUE	PERCENTAGE INCREASE OR DECREASE
1. $105,000	8%	1. $96,600	(–3.4%)
2. $110,250	7%	2. $102,532	2.30%
3. $115,763	6%	3. $108,817	8.81%
4. $121,551	5%	4. $115,474	15.47%
5. $127,628	4%	5. $122,523	22.52%
6. $134,010	3%	6. $129,990	29.99%
7. $140,710	2%	7. $137,896	37.90%
8. $147,746	1%	8. $146,269	46.27%
9. $155,132	0%	9. $155,132	55.00%

The fourth column in above chart calculates the percentage increase or decrease in the initial premium based on a total surrender each year. For example, if they surrendered at the end of the first year, an 8% surrender charge imposed on the total hypothetical value would have resulted in a Cash Surrender Value of $96,600, a –3.4% decrease on the initial $100,000 premium. If the annuity contract waived surrender charges for a 10% partial withdrawal preceding a surrender, the above percentage decrease would be less and increases would be even greater for the annuity owner.

The above chart assumes a $100,000 premium, a hypothetical annuity crediting an interest rate of 5% each year, 8 year surrender charge period with a surrender charge of 8% in year one decreasing 1% each year to 0% in year 9 with no market value adjustment. In actuality, interest rates vary by product and carrier and all parties should see the insurer disclosure and annuity contract for guaranteed interest rates, values, surrender charges and a market value adjustment, if any. Guarantees are subject to the claims paying ability of the particular insurer.

9 *You can overcome any objection about surrender charges if you use this material.*

Surrender Charge Quiz

1. Surrender charges exist to

   a) protect an insurer from a run on the bank

   b) be able to pay respectable commissions

   c) both of the above

2. Showing the annuity that you own

   a) is discouraged by almost everyone

   b) is recommended by W.V.H., Inc.

   c) is not allowed by any insurer

3. True or False

   Almost every financial product has a surrender penalty of some kind.

Answers

1. c 2. b 3. True

You can get up to 80% of the seminar audience to want to get together with you.

As reported earlier on page 113, we need to do 3 things to do to have "exceptional seminar success". First, we need to be likeable. Second, we need to give them 2-3 unforgettable ideas. Third, we need to convince them that we can help them. The special questionnaire on the next page convinces them that they need you. You are one page away from getting up to 80% of the "buying units " at your seminar to want to get together with you.

10 *You can get up to 80% of the seminar audience to want to get together with you.*

Special Questionnaire

The purpose of the seminar is for them to decide whether or not you can help them.

We call the questionnaire special only because it works. You can use any questionnaire as long as you use it the right way. For example, at the end of your 45 minute seminar, you pass out this special questionnaire. The first two questions on the questionnaire are important. The first question is, "Did you find this seminar informative?" (Everyone is going to say, "Yes".) The second question is, "Would you like to be invited to more seminars?"

We are doing something very important here. We are getting the attendees in the routine of completing this form. We then move to the section of this questionnaire where you have the needs listed: Social Security, More Money Later, Tax–Advantaged Income, Inflation, etc. It is how you use this section of the questionnaire that could determine the amount of business you'll eventually write. Simply put, you do a quick commercial on how you can solve each particular need. Here is an example of what you could say at the seminar.

> "Many of you are upset about paying taxes on your Social Security income. I don't blame you. We have a special form." (Hold it up, put it down.) "It takes only 3 minutes to complete. Many of you are paying taxes unnecessarily. If you wish to potentially reduce or eliminate this tax, please make a check mark next to Social Security on this questionnaire."

Did I teach anyone in the audience how I solve that need or do they just know that I can do it? The purpose of a seminar is not to train every attendee on how every need can be solved. They are only interested in their needs. The purpose of the seminar is for them to decide whether or not you can help them. You either convince them that you can help them or they convince you that you cannot help them.

Customer Seminar Questionnaire

1. I found the seminar informative

2. I would like to be invited to more seminars
   in the future

Needs that are most important to me:

☐ A. Receiving a guaranteed stream of income for life.

☐ B. Reducing current taxes but still enjoying access to
   my money.

☐ C. Accumulating more money for myself or heirs.

☐ D. Reducing or eliminating taxes on Social Security
   benefits.

☐ E. Overcoming the erosion of my purchasing power
   because of inflation.

Name: _____

Mailing Address: _____

_____

_____

Phone# : _____

Best time to call: _____

10 *You can get up to 80% of the seminar audience to want to get together with you.*

Homework Assignment

Seminars

List all the reasons why seminar attendees should want to get together with you.

1. *You can help them reduce the income tax they are paying on their Social Security Income*

2. _____
   _____.

3. _____
   _____.

4. _____
   _____.

5. _____
   _____.

6. _____
   _____.

7. _____
   _____.

8. _____
   _____.

9. _____
   _____.

10. _____
   _____.

secret **11**

You can use this formula for success.

F ortunately, it does not take much to reach the next level of success in any profession. In baseball, the difference between a batter batting .250 and .333 is one base hit a week. In golf, the difference between the #1 golfer and the #10 golfer was slightly over 1 stroke per 18 holes. (and 84 million dollars in prize money). While this secret will not generate 84 millions dollars in commissions, it can take you the next level.

11 *You can use this formula for success.*

Increase Your Success In the Profession Of Selling

Know your position

If we are in the profession of selling insurance products, we are in the profession of helping. All we have to do is ask customers what they want and we will help them get what they want. We just have to ask. Fortunately, there are additional ways for you to increase your level of success fairly easily.

You have already begun the first way of upgrading your level of
success by reading this book. You want to learn more about your
profession. You want to know the best ways to market, to prospect, to fact–find, to present, and to close. You want to create a strong basic foundation of knowledge about the field of selling insurance products.

Selling Tip # 1 Rehearse your presentation, your close, your new ways to overcome objections. This can be done at home or in the car, but not when you are sitting across the desk from a person who has $250,000.

Your customer comes first. You come last.

The second way of increasing your level of success is by creating your own formula. What do I mean? Recognize which characteristics, traits, and habits of yours deliver results and stick with those. For example, I'll share with you the formula that I have used. You may wish to add some of these to your formula.

BE CREDIBLE. Know your competition and know how you compare. It is your profession. If another company has a feature superior to yours, recognize that the feature is superior, but also accentuate your other strengths.

BE POSITIVE. Never say anything bad about a competitor. Never. Present your strengths. The customer will compare.

BE DIFFERENT. I always evaluate what others are doing and, more importantly, what they are not doing. When you are different, it is more difficult to be compared, isn't it?

BE PROUD. Know your profession well. Attempt to know your product better than anyone else.

BE AMBITIOUS. 40 hours a week is perfect for anyone who is happy with their current economic status. Otherwise, use math to your advantage. Increase your income 14% (work Saturdays). Increase your income 100% (work 80 hours a week). We once celebrated the introduction of a new annuity by opening the office at 6:00 AM and closing at midnight.

BE A TEAM PLAYER. Place your client and their needs first, then your employees, then your needs. Ironically, the person who places himself last always really wins.

You can use this formula for success.

You will be truly convincing only after you are convinced.

In the profession of selling, you must be convinced before you can be convincing. For example, let's assume that you do not own an annuity because it is not insured by the government. Let's further assume that you are giving an annuity presentation to a prospect who has $250,000. In fact, during the latter stage of your presentation, your prospect pulled his checkbook out and started filling in the date and the amount. Your presentation is now over and the prospect says, "It would be nice if the annuity were insured by the government, wouldn't it?"

Allow me to tell you what now happens. If you are not totally convinced, there is a little part of your brain that will always say to you whenever a customer makes that response, "I know what you mean. I wish the annuity were insured, too." How can you be convincing if you are not convinced!

Suggestion: You should own the same annuity that you are selling. This allows you to say, "Mr. Jones, I also have dollars that I wanted to accumulate faster with security. The annuity that I'm discussing with you today (now take your annuity policy out) is where I have my money."

If you really want to increase your closing ratio, sell your Mom an annuity. Then you can say, "Mr. Jones, the annuity I'm recommending to you is the same annuity that I sold to my Mom." This will accomplish two benefits: 1) your closing ratio will dramatically improve, 2) your Mom can have potentially more money later because she owns an annuity.

Is there anything else that will improve your level of success? Yes, the words that you use in your delivery are critical to your success. Are there special words that are more effective than others? Yes, this book is full of power phrases, buzz words, button–down questions, and test closes that have consistently delivered success. However, you can increase your level of success by using superlatives and the word guaranteed whenever possible. In fact, we have examples on the opposite page.

5 SUPERLATIVES

1. "You think the greatest benefit is the guaranteed minimum value, don't you?" (or use access to your money or tax deferral instead).

2. "In your opinion, Mr. Jones, which can accumulate fastest: a CD, a Treasury bill, or an annuity?"

3. "The insurance company that you are selecting is one of the oldest, one of the largest, and one of the most respected insurance companies in America."

4. "This insurance company is the most dominant player in the annuity marketplace."

5. "You can select any annuity from among the finest companies in America." (Or use oldest or largest in place of finest.)

   Is there anything else you can do that will increase results for you? YES, use the word guarantee (if they are guaranteed in the annuity contract) whenever possible and watch your level of success increase.

GUARANTEED AND GUARANTEE

1. "You receive 5% guaranteed for one year."

2. "You are guaranteed that your annuity value will be $105,000 next year, guaranteed."

3. "You are guaranteed no initial sales charges nor any annual fees."

4. "Surrender charges will disappear after 6 years. And, they will not reappear, guaranteed."

5. "If you wish, you can receive guaranteed monthly income. We can guarantee that it will continue for life. If you wish, we can even guarantee 10 years, 15 years, or 20 years of payments."

6. "You also receive an interest rate guaranteed for the life of the annuity."

7. "You have a guaranteed selling price every year."

11

You can use this formula for success.

Wouldn't it be nice if you could get prospects to tell you that they want the benefits of owning an annuity? Just ask these important questions and write down their answers.

> "Mr. Jones, practically all of my customers are smart because they have accounts like these (point toward top of page). With regard to your accounts here, are you leaving the interest in or taking the interest out? (fill in answer).
>
> What do you like most about these accounts? Is it security? (fill in answer).
>
> Do you need these dollars in one, two, or three years or do you just want access to these dollars here if an emergency arises? (fill in answer).
>
> Specifically (pointing to the word CD), what interest rate are you receiving here? (fill in answer). How much longer will you be enjoying that rate? (fill in maturity date). Are you also receiving that interest rate on this money market account? (await response). No, what are you receiving? (fill in answer and repeat this pattern of questioning for their passbook savings).
>
> Other than security, access, and a choice of interest rate guarantee periods, is there anything else you like about these accounts? (await response).
>
> Which extra benefits do you wish your bank accounts had? (don't pause). I'm sure a higher return (pause for nod) and less income taxes on your interest (await favorable response).
>
> If I am reading you correctly, and I think I am, you want security, access to your money, choice of interest rates, a higher return, and less current income taxes. Am I reading you correctly?"

Yes, they have asked you for an annuity. Please give to them what they want. When you start giving them what they want, you start getting what you want.

Would you like to learn how to get prospects

| CERTIFICATE OF DEPOSIT MONEY MARKET ACCOUNTS PASSBOOK SAVINGS | CERTIFICATE OF DEPOSIT MONEY MARKET ACCOUNTS PASSBOOK SAVINGS |

1. Are you leaving the interest in or taking out the interest?

    ☐ IN   ☐ OUT

2. What do you like MOST about these savings accounts?

    _____

    _____

Security	Access
☐ YES ☐ NO	☐ In__years ☐ If an Emergency Arises

Interest Rates	Other features important to you
RATE ___% ___% ___%	_____
DURATION	_____
___ ___ ___	

3. What extra BENEFITS do you wish your savings account had?

Higher Return	Less income taxes on interest
☐ YES ☐ NO	☐ YES ☐ NO

. . . to tell you where all of their bank money is and when it matures? What if you could get prospects to ask you for an annuity? All of the above can be done during the first 60 seconds if you use this special form the right way.

11 *You can use this formula for success.*

You now know the easy, yet important ways to increase your level of success.

1. Be willing to grow professionally by sharpening your selling skills.
2. Develop your own formula.
3. Be convincing and carry your annuity with you.
4. Use superlatives whenever possible.
5. Add the word guarantee to your delivery for guaranteed results.
6. Use that special fact–finding form at the onset.

Success Quiz

1. True or False (please circle)

   The profession of selling is also the profession of helping.

2. Whose needs should be placed ahead of yours?

   a) your clients
   b) your prospects
   c) your employees
   d) all of the above

3. For you to be convincing, you need

   a) the best product in the industry
   b) to feel relaxed
   c) to be convinced

Answers: 1. True 2. d 3. c

You can find new annuity dollars by using the right approach

Not too long ago, we were contracted to teach one large group of investment professionals how to get dollars from the bank. Sales doubled. On the following pages, we unveil a special way to find bank dollars by using a similar but better approach. You are one page away from learning how to potentially double your annuity commissions by using the right words with the right approach. Want to turn the page?

12 *You can find new annuity dollars by using the right approach.*

Introduction to Approach

In 1400 B.C., Prince Hepd'efal purchased an annuity. Believe or not, it was NOT as a result of a 1035 tax-free exchange, IRA Rollover or IRA Transfer.

Unfortunately, a very high percentage of "new" annuity business is a result of 1035 exchanges, IRA Rollovers, and IRA Transfers.

In the Annuity Fact Book, NAVA accurately points out that withdrawal and surrender activity and 1035 exchanges "either does not result in new dollars to the industry (exchanges) or drains dollars from the industry (withdrawals and surrenders)".

In our opinion, too many of the dollars going to annuities last year came from the pockets of other insurance companies. While most of the exchanges were in the consumer's best interests, we wonder if we are collectively strengthening our industry and our profession.

Would our industry be stronger if insurers were not subject to so many exchanges, roll overs, and transfers each year?

Could actuaries then design annuities with even more pro-consumer benefits if persistency improved?

Wouldn't compliance, FINRA, and state departments of insurance like knowing that less policyholders incurred surrender charges at the time of exchanges, roll overs or transfers?

And, would insurance and investment professionals be able to build stronger careers if we discovered better ways to find bank dollars from existing annuity owners instead of moving annuity dollars from one insurer to another?

2 Important Facts

Fact #1 How many dollars are out there?

Before you use our new common sense approach to finding bank dollars from existing annuity owners, are there enough bank dollars out there?

According to a conversation we had with the Federal Reserve and the chart they faxed to us, Certificates of Deposit, Passbook Savings, and Money Market Accounts owned by individuals is close to 5.9 TRILLION dollars!!!

If 80% of the $255 billion in variable and fixed annuity sales came from the pockets of other insurers, that means we got only 51 billion dollars from the 5.9 TRILLION DOLLAR bank vault last year. In other words, we—embarrassingly—got less than one penny of every bank dollar in spite of us having tax-deferred growth, lifetime income, death benefit guarantees, and the advantage to having a surrender charge period.

Said differently, in spite of us being "the only franchise in the financial world" that can provide guaranteed income for life, we got less than one penny from every bank dollar.

So, the money is there. And, if this secret helps you get only 2 cents from every bank dollar, we have just helped you DOUBLE your income. Far more importantly, we can help thousands of consumers potentially achieve the financial and emotional independence they want and deserve.

(Continued on next page)

You can find new annuity dollars by using the right approach.

(Introduction to approach continued)

Fact # 2 How does the annuity owner feel about themselves at the point of sale?

Let's assume that your clients and prospects have met 10 different insurance and investment professionals since they purchased their annuity(ies). During those 10 meetings with the insurance and investment professionals, what percentage of the time do you think your clients and prospects heard that they purchased "the wrong type" of annuity or "the old kind of annuity" or "an annuity with the wrong insurer"?

Do you think that your clients and prospects felt smart after hearing about their annuity shopping skills? Or, did they feel dumb, duped, or mad?

New Approach To Finding New Dollars

The next time that you meet a prospect or client who owns an annuity, please consider saying this:

> "Steve, 10 years ago, when you were 50, you made a very wise decision when you purchased an annuity. Because of that smart decision you made 10 years ago, you diversified your money, paid less income taxes on the earnings and, as a result, you now have more money. Smart decision, Steve.
>
> In fact, if you had needed money during the last 10 years, you could have received guaranteed income for life or for a period of years by annuitizing your annuity. Or, you could have withdrawn 10% of your annuity value during the surrender charge period and withdrawn 100% of your annuity value after the surrender charge period without any insurance company penalties. Naturally, you would have paid taxes on the tax-deferred earnings withdrawn.

Steve, 10 years ago, you made a very wise decision. It is now time to make another wise decision. Let's now look at some of the money that you have at the bank and let's get some of the those dollars accumulating on a tax-deferred basis. Why pay income taxes on earnings you do not quite yet need? Sounds like a good idea again, doesn't it?"

Summary

Let's strengthen our industry and our profession by learning how to find new dollars from existing annuity owners. If we do, we will be well on our way to helping our clients achieve the financial and emotional independence they want and need.

12 *You can find new annuity dollars by using the right approach.*

Quiz

1. What % of CD money is repositioned to annuities each year?

   a) 10%

   b) 20%

   c) 5%

   d) 1%

2. Consumers who are constantly told they bought the wrong type of annuity can get

   a) irritated

   b) upset

   c) less apt to be receptive

   d) all of the above

secret

You can learn a lot from history.

A s you are well aware, history plays an important part of every college curriculum. While history does not affect the future, history helps all of us grasp relevant issues. History also plays an important role in the financial services industry.

What makes this secret so special is that many lessons can be embraced by reading what former Presidents of the United States have said about the economy, income taxes, inflation, and Social Security.

Presidents of the United States | 245

13 *You can learn a lot from history.*

If every insurance and investment professional and consumer had learned or remembered each of the following facts, imagine how much richer so many of them would be today.

Problem The stock market goes up but also goes down.

Solution It would be wise to have some products in your portfolio that can help you when either occurs.

Problem Inflation can be dormant but can re-ignite.

Solution Tax-deferred accumulation can help you have more dollars later just in case.

Problem There will probably always be bear markets and bull markets.

Solution Diversification can soften the impact of a bear market and assist you in a bull market.

Problem Interest rates go up and also go down.

Solution It is smart to diversify your dollars among a variety of products, some that perform well during an increasing interest rate environment and some that perform well during a decreasing rate environment.

Problem Social Security was never intended to be a major source of retirement income.

Solution Planning for retirement gives you new sources for income.

Problem Never put all of your money in one place.

Solution Diversification makes good business sense.

> Since we are "Solutionists", use history to help you pinpoint potential problems. And, use your professional education, seasoning, and books like ours to formulate solutions.
>
> In this secret, you learn which Presidents said, "The power to tax is the power to destroy", "Yesterday, the stock market went up more than it ever has in history, over 35 points", "The Social Security program was initially predicated on the basis that it was not to be your total retirement income, but as a base or a floor."
>
> On our *75 Secrets* Audio CDs and DVD-ROMs, you'll be able to see and or hear former Presidents of the United States talk about the topics we discuss everyday. However, they do it in a special unforgettable way.

13 *You can learn a lot from history.*

THE ECONOMY

Dwight Eisenhower: "Now, I am not saying that the stock market itself, its rises and falls, is necessarily an index of what is going to happen in this country; but it does reflect the confidence that we have tried in the past so hard to instill."

John F. Kennedy: "For the first time in history, we have 70 million men and women that work. For the first time in history, factory earnings have exceeded $100 a week and even the stock market has broken all records, though we only get credit when it goes down."

Jimmy Carter: "As you know, day before yesterday, the stock market went up more than it ever has in history, over 35 points."

Ronald Reagan: "Inflation is at its lowest level in more than a decade. The economy has been creating new jobs at a note of hundreds of thousands each month. Just this week, the Dow Jones Industrial Average broke 1300, a new record, and the New York Daily News carried a headline that I will always cherish. It simply read Zippity-Do- Dow."

George H. W. Bush: "Just the past couple of months, consumer confidence has soared. And, the stock market, of course, has been climbing toward that 3000 mark."

Jimmy Carter: "As you know, day before yesterday, the stock market went up more than it ever has in history, over 35 points."

Photo courtesy of : Jimmy Carter Presidential Library

You can learn a lot from history.

INCOME TAXES

Again, from an historical perspective, we learn more about income taxes from the "mind-set" of American Presidents over the past 60 years.

Franklin D. Roosevelt: "Today, I have advised the Congress of the importance of speeding up the passage of the tax bill. Taxation is the only practical way of preventing the incomes and profits of individuals and corporations from getting too high."

John F. Kennedy: "This net reduction in tax liabilities of $10 billion will increase the purchasing power of American families and business enterprises in every tax bracket for the greatest increase going to our low-income consumers."

Lyndon B. Johnson: "And the most damaging and devastating thing you can do to any businessman in America is to keep him in doubt and to keep him guessing on what our tax policy is."

Gerald Ford: "This country needs an immediate federal income tax cut of $16 billion ...$12 billion, or three-fourths of the total of this cut, should go to individual tax payers in the form of a cash rebate."

Jimmy Carter: "The bill must be simple, fair, equitable, progressive in nature—that is, putting the tax burden where people can most afford it. And, the substantial reduction in tax burden on our people, if it meets those requirements, then, I will sign it."

Ronald Reagan: "Yet, past government policies betrayed families and family values. They permitted inflation to push families relentlessly in higher and higher tax brackets, and not only did the personal exemption fail to keep pace with inflation in real dollars, its actual value dropped dramatically over the last 30 years. The power to tax is the power to destroy."

Lyndon B. Johnson: "And the most damaging and devastating thing you can do to any businessman in America is to keep him in doubt and to keep him guessing on what our tax policy is."

Photo courtesy of: Lyndon Baines Johnson Presidential Library

13 *You can learn a lot from history.*

One of the needs that we should often discuss is overcoming inflation. However, the consumer is now saying that inflation is "under control." Therefore, we need a way to show clients that we've always had inflation, and you know something, we probably always will. One of the best ways to show that inflation is always "active" or "dormant" is by using history. Here, we show what Presidents of the past have said about inflation.

INFLATION

Franklin D. Roosevelt: "Some call it inflation . . . From January 1, 1941 to May of this year, nearly a year and a half, the cost of living went up about 15 percent."

Dwight Eisenhower: "As I recall, since the last raise in minimum wage to 75 cents, there had been a total rise in that time in the cost of living to justify a minimum wage of something on the order of 85.6 or 86.5, and we took the 90 cents as a good leveling-off figure and that was the way we arrived at it."

John F. Kennedy: "There has been a steady inflationary rise throughout the history of the United States."

Lyndon B. Johnson: "And, before long we'll all get hurt as inflation eats away at the foundations of our economy. A man could build a house in 1946 for $10,000 and that house costs more than $20,000 today."

Jimmy Carter: "Inflation will soar; production will go down; people will lose their jobs."

Ronald Reagan: "Inflation is like a virus in the economic bloodstream . . . sometimes dormant and sometimes active, but leaving the patient weaker after every new attack."

Ronald Reagan: "Inflation is like a virus in the economic bloodstream . . . sometimes dormant and sometimes active, but leaving the patient weaker after every new attack."

Photo courtesy of: Ronald Reagan Presidential Library

13 *You can learn a lot from history.*

SOCIAL SECURITY

Another need we often discuss with consumers is Social Security. Unfortunately, too many of our clients "over depend" on the Social Security program. One way to show the importance of people "depending less upon the Social Security program" is to show historically what Presidents of the Past have said about Social Security.

Franklin D. Roosevelt: "And, that is why our Social Security program is an important part of the complete picture. It proposes, by means of old age pension, to help those who have reached the age of retirement to give up their jobs and thus give to the younger generation greater opportunities for work. And, to give to all, old and young alike, a feeling of security as they look towards old age."

John F. Kennedy: "I have sent to the Congress today a message of the needs of our 17-½ billion senior citizens. The number of people in this country age 65 and over increases by one thousand every day as science prolongs the life span. But, it's not enough for a great nation merely to add to the years of lives, our object also must be to add to new life to those years."

Gerald Ford: "The Social Security program, which became law in 1933 or 34, as I recall, was initially predicated on the basis that it was not to be your total retirement income, but as a base or a floor."

Jimmy Carter: "One of the things that we had to do last year was to bring the Social Security system out of near bankruptcy into a sound economic position. Two of the three major reserve funds for the Social Security were on the verge of bankruptcy."

Ronald Reagan: "To all of you listening, and particularly those of you now receiving Social Security, I ask you to listen very carefully. Some thirty years ago, there were 16 people working and paying the Social Security payroll tax for everyone retiring. Today, that ratio is changed to only 3.2 workers paying in for each beneficiary."

Gerald Ford: "The Social Security program, which became law in 1933 or 34, as I recall, was initially predicated on the basis that it was not to be your total retirement income, but as a base or a floor."

Photo courtesy of: Gerald R. Ford Presidential Library

Presidential Quiz

Who Said

1. "I recommend that the tax treatment of annuities be determined on the basis of the life expectancy of the person receiving it. This will permit the hundreds of thousands of people who by ANNUITIES to recover their capital free of tax over their life expectancies."

2. "Might not be both competent and expedient for Congress to provide that a limited amount of some future issues of public securities might be held by any bona fide purchaser exempt from taxation and from seizure for debt:, "This would enable every prudent person to set aside a small ANNUITY against a possible day of want."

3. "Employees who want to establish their own retirement plan should be offered a tax incentive comparable to that now given those in group rate plans. Individuals could retain the power to control the investment of these funds channeling them into qualified ban accounts, mutual funds, ANNUITY or insurance programs."

4. "Instead of giving them stock which may be passed into other hands and render them the prey of speculators, an ANNUITY shall be paid them."

Answers: 1. Dwight D. Eisenhower 2. Abraham Lincon 3. Richard M. Nixon 4. Thomas Jefferson

14

You can have more success if you have these words on your business card.

F or those who have attended our live speaking engagements and or live web conferences, you already know that I use the business card as a symbol to discuss our "value" to consumers. On the following pages, we discuss our "value" of asking people what they want and helping people think about their money on a regular basis by using the business card as a symbol. We hope you like it.

14 *You can have more success if you have these words on your business card.*

Business Cards #1

Wouldn't it be nice if something as simple as changing your business card could change your career? Before we describe how to change the back of your business card, let's discuss if you should change your card. Please take one of your business cards out and take a good look at it. Does your card really describe what you do for a living? How does your card describe you? Imagine the back of your business card saying some of the following:

"I ask people what they want, and I help them get what they want. If you could sit down with me for 10 minutes and tell me what you want, I can help you get what you want.

- Do you want the best health insurance for your family? I can help.

- Do you want insurance to pick-up where Medicare leaves off? I can help.

- Do you want to protect the people you love? I can help.

- Do you want to insure your mortgage? I can help.

- Do you want your family to maintain their lifestyle if something happens to you? I can help.

- Do you want more dollars for retirement? I can help.

- Do you want more dollars for your heirs? I can help.

- Do you want more money for emergencies and opportunities? I can help.

- Do you want to have money when it is needed the most… at disability…at retirement…and at death? I can help.

- Do you want your child to go to college? I can help.

- Do you want a check the first of every month for as long as you live? I can help."

Please tell me what you want, and I can help you get what you want.

Note: Please show your insurance companies and Broker Dealer any changes you want made to your business card.

Business Card #2

The next time you are asked what you do for a living, we would like you to say "I help people think about their money on a regular basis."

Friends, that is what we do more than anything else.

Unfortunately, people do not think about their money on a regular basis. If they did, would they really have $2,000 of credit card debt paying interest rates of 18%-22% when they have $2,000 tucked away at the bank earning 1%? If they thought about their money regularly, they would get that $2,000 at the bank and pay off that $2,000 of credit card debt and immediately be 17%-21% richer.

One of the greatest things that insurance and investment professionals do when they get together with consumers is to help them think about their money on a regular basis. When we were all growing up, our parents told us never to put all of our eggs in one basket. But, in spite of that, too many of us still put too much of our money in one given product or concept. Therefore, one of the major responsibilities of an insurance and investment professional is to help consumers think about their money before they retire and during their retirement.

The bottom line is that they owe it to their spouse, to their children and, maybe, to their grandchildren to be the best that they can be. And, thinking about their money regularly is their job. However, you can help...and, adding the following words to your business card makes a great deal of sense. "I help people think about their money on a regular basis."

14 *You can have more success if you have these words on your business card.*

Homework Assignment

List all of the ways that you can help people.

1. *Help them pay taxes later instead of now.*

2. _____

3. _____

4. _____

5. _____

6. _____

7. _____

8. _____

9. _____

10. _____

The Next 30 Days: Your New Way To Fill Your Prospecting Pipeline

And, just when you thought you were done reading our book, we surprise you with one career-enhancing activity to do every business day of the year. But, before we explain this section, allow me to tell you how this section evolved. Every so often, we offer "FREE" mentoring services to those clients who own all of our products. During a very recent mentoring session, I became totally convinced that some of us need detailed direction, guidance, and sometimes, a "to do" list. On the following 30 pages, we not only ask you to call 5 people, we gently and respectfully tell you PRECISELY who to call that day.

Rules Before You Begin

Rule #1: Please do NOT read ahead. Read only one page every day. OK?

Rule #2: For the first 7 days, please call those people we ask you to call. After 7 days, if this section did not help you fill your prospecting pipeline, you can read ahead, go back, and look for the easy ones. Is that fair? I am just trying to help you and I know I can.

Homework

One more homework assignment, but you will not need to have this assignment done until you get to Day 20. Hire a high school or college student and ask them to go to your file cabinet and create an Excel sheet with the following categories: 1) names of all of your clients, former clients, and current prospects, 2) the type they are like (c) for clients, (fc) for former clients and (cp) for current prospects, 3) their date of birth, 4) their occupation and industry, like doctor/ medicine, and 5) the date of the first application that you ever completed for that client or former client; just the first application.

Since statistics show that owners of this book either already own or will soon order *75 Secrets; An Insider's Guide to Bank CDs, Annuities, & Retirement Planning*, we tell you on the bottom of each page where to the find the best sales-creating words, charts, or questionnaires for the 5 people we are asking you to call. As you will soon see, reaching out to the right prospects and converting those prospects to clients just got a lot easier.

Are you ready to begin filling your prospecting pipeline today? Then, quickly turn the page. If you are not ready to begin, then turn the page tomorrow. OK?

Day 1

Call 5 former clients.

They know you. They like you. They respect you. They just got sidetracked a few years ago and turned to someone else.

Suggest that:

1. they are only as strong as the people and advisors that surround them

2. you do not want to replace any of their current advisors

3. you DO want to be part of their financial support team again, especially now because of the new ways you can help them*

*If they ask you the new ways, quickly turn to the table of contents in *75 Secrets,* list as many of the 75 new ways as you can in 10 seconds.

Day 2

Call 5 of your current prospects who have an IRA.

Show them how a non-qualified annuity picks up where their IRA leaves off.

Some of the things you will be comparing:

1. Similar tax-deferred accumulation

2. Similar 10% excise tax penalty

3. Dramatically different maximum premium

4. Dramatically different forced distribution penalty (50% vs. none)

Please look at Secret 55 in our book *75 Secrets,* pages 219-222 with the complete comparison and the best point-of-sale words.

Day 3

Call 5 of your former clients who think term life insurance is better.

Show them all 4 reasons why term is not always best.

Some of the things you will be discussing:

1. Longer life expectancy*

2. Term premiums for people 60-75 years old

3. The difficulty many have "investing the difference"*

4. The 40% loss that many who did "invest the difference" had in 2008

*Please re-read pages 87 & 88 in this book regarding overcoming objections about buying term and investing the difference. Please look at our *75 Secrets* book: Secret 10 page 39 for life expectancy estimates and Secret 40 page 160 for how little people save.

Day 4

Call 5 of your current clients who want insurance, but who think they cannot afford it.

Show them how to redirect the money they are spending on less important things to far more important things.

Some of the things you will be discussing:

1. How a cup of coffee every day can cost them $43,580 if they remain a spender*

2. Which things are most important: a triple pounder, a cup of joe, pack of cigarettes, or college for the children

*Please look at Secret 29 in our book *75 Secrets* page 117 for a chart showing what life's indulgences really cost.

Day 5

Call 5 people you know who probably lost 40% of their money in 2008.

Show them how to reposition "some of their money" into a product that can guarantee what their money will be worth every year.

Some of the things you will be discussing:

1. Importance of diversification

2. The advantages and disadvantages of annuities*

3. Why surrender charges are a major plus*

4. How to get a % of the gains in an external index*

*Please look at Secrets 61, 64, 67 for great info about surrender charges, Secrets 69 & 71 about Indexed Annuities and pages 329-336 for advantages & disadvantages.

Day 6

Call 5 people you know who are receiving Social Security & who are most apt to be paying income taxes on that income.

Show them how to reposition "some of their money" into an annuity or life product so they can potentially reduce or eliminate the income taxes they are paying on their Social Security income.

Some of the things you will be discussing:

1. Why pay income taxes on taxable interest you do not yet need?

2. Tax control with an annuity

3. Our special Social Security questionnaire*

---

*Please look at Secrets 53 pages 211-214, the hypothetical questionnaire on page 213, and the 2 Social Security questionnaires you can print and distribute to their tax advisors on pages 240-241.

Day 7

Call 5 people you know who either own or who are thinking about owning Municipal Bonds.

Show them the disadvantages and advantages.

Some of the things you will be discussing:

1. What happens to Muni Bonds when interest rates rise

2. The probability to where future interest rates may be going

3. Muni Bonds that are callable

4. The claims paying ability of bond issuer

*Please look at our 75 Secrets book: Secret 36 titled "Tax free may not be as good as you think." on pages. 143-146 and the chart on page 145 that accurately shows what some bond holders lost during the last major increasing interest rate environment.

Day 8

Call 5 people who already own an annuity.

Remind them they made a wise decision, tell them why it was a wise decision, and tell them again that it is time to make another wise decision.

Show them how they have benefited such as:

1. Less income taxes

2. More money now

3. Access to 10 % of their money during the surrender charge period and 100% access to their money after the surrender charge period.

4 The choice of electing guaranteed income for life

Please re-read pages in this book on pages 242-243 for the best phone script. In the *75 Secrets* book, look at Secrets 61, 64, 67 for great info about surrender charges, and pages 329-336 for advantages & disadvantages for all types of annuities.

Day 9

Call 5 of your clients who have children who are married.

You have been very helpful to your clients and they will correctly assume that you can be helpful to their children too.

Some of the ways you can help:

1. Protecting the people they love with life insurance

2. Mortgage protection

3. Reducing debt via mentoring or paying off debt at death with life insurance

4. Importance of them paying themselves first

5. Keeping their grocery bag full even when disabled via disability income

Day 10

Call 5 accountants who work with your clients.

You both share the same client. Tell them you just bought a $75 book that will help you help your clients. On page 185, the book unveils how some taxpayers can reduce the effective tax rate by 33.9%.

Say the following:

"I respect your opinion and I would like to know if this idea can help not only our client, but your other clients as well."

Please read Secret 46 in *75 Secrets* titled *An annuity can lower your Modified Adjusted Gross Income, tax bracket, and get you tax deductions (previously disallowed)*

Day 11

Call 5 business owners who work on Saturdays.

Tell them you would like to stop by next Saturday, give them the IRS brochure 5305 SEP, and show them how they can slash what they pay in income taxes by opening a Simplified Employee Pension Plan with a bank, insurance company, or mutual fund.

Naturally re-read the Secret #2 in this book titled *Using The Phone* and Secret #41 in *75 Secrets* titled *You can make a tax-deductible contribution of $49,000 if you own a business.* Please pay particular attention to all the ways that a small business owner can exclude some or all employees.

Day 12

Call 5 people you know that have money in the bank.

Tell them that you just bought a $75 book that will help you help your clients. On page 15, the book shows a chart from the Federal Reserve that surprisingly shows that while CDs protect CD owners from risk to principal, CDs do NOT protect CD owners from interest rate risk.

1. Suggest that they have to see this chart

2. Ask where the best place is to meet

Please read Secret 4 titled *CD interest rates are far more volatile than you think*, pages 13-16 in the *75 Secrets* book.

Day 13

Call 5 of your clients who have parents.

You have been very helpful to your clients and they will correctly assume that you can be helpful to their parents too.

Some of the ways you can help:

1. Reducing income taxes on their Social Security Income.*

2 Long Term Care Insurance

3. Reducing debt via mentoring or paying off debt at death with life insurance

*Please look at Secret 53 in our book *75 Secrets,* pages. 211-214 with special attention to the questionnaire on page 213 that can help you reduce taxes on Social Security Income.

Day 14

Call 5 people who strongly feel that a variable annuity is vastly superior to a fixed annuity (or vice versa).

Share with them:

- that you just bought a $75 book that will help you help your clients

- the name of the book

- that pp. 195-198 unveil Secret #49, which is titled *You can select the best type of annuity if you diversify.*

Tell them that they have to see this book.

Suggest to meet for 15 minutes at their favorite coffee shop tomorrow morning.

The bottom line: You can now make sure that 50% of their money goes into the 2 best types of annuities and that 100% of their annuity money never goes into the wrong type. Why? Because you care!

Day 15

Call 5 people who might want both guaranteed income and tax-deferred accumulation.

Share with them:

- that you just bought a $75 book that will help you help your clients

- the name of the book

- that pp. 227-230 unveil Secret # 57 which is titled *You can now get tax-deferral and monthly income at the same time if you know how to shop.*

Tell them that they have to see this book.

Suggest to meet for 15 minutes at their favorite coffee shop tomorrow morning.

Day 16

Call 5 people who are most apt to have more than $100,000 in an IRA.

Share with them:

• that in 2010 for the first time ever they can—regardless to income—generate a stream of tax-free income for themselves,children, and grandchildren

• it is called a ROTH IRA

• that almost everyone is recommending this, BUT a new $75 book that you just bought says it could be either a big mistake or the best thing you ever do. In fact, the book lists the 4 things they should consider first—

Tell them that they have to see this book.

Suggest to meet for 15 minutes at their favorite ice cream shop tomorrow evening.

Day 17

Call 5 people who are grandparents.

Share with them:

- that you just bought a $75 book that will help you help your clients

- tell them the name of the book

- that pp. 91-94 unveil Secret # 23, which is titled *A one-time $2,000 gift to a baby born today could be worth $1,000,000 at retirement*

Share with them that they were one of the first 5 people you thought of this morning who are most apt to want to help their grandchildren.

Ask them the best place to meet for 15 minutes tomorrow—local library, their place, or a coffee shop nearby.

Day 18

Call 5 seasoned small business owners "you know" who work on Sunday.

Share with them why you would like to stop by next Sunday:

• that you just bought a $75 book that will help you help your clients

• tell them the name of the book and that

• pp. 251-254 unveil Secret # 63, which is titled *A 412(i) pension plan is the most overlooked buying opportunity by small business owners*

Share with them that they were one of the first 5 people you thought of this morning who are most apt to want to take advantage of this secret and make LARGE tax deductible contributions for their retirement.

Ask them for the best time to stop by for 15 minutes on Sunday and if they want you to bring coffee and donuts at 7:30 AM?

Day 19

Call 5 people age 50 and older who you know who are more apt to have a 401(k) at work.

Share with them:

- that you just bought a $75 book that will help you help your clients

- tell them the name of the book

- pp. 99-102 unveil Secret # 25, which is titled *The IRS allows people age 50 and older to catch up and contribute an extra $5,500 to their 401(k)*

Share with them that "they" were among the first 5 people you thought of this morning who are most apt to want to take advantage of this secret and accumulate more money for a nicer retirement.

Ask them if they want to meet you at their favorite ice cream shop (smile in voice) so you can discuss the 3 tax flavors of saving: taxable, tax-deferred, and tax-free.

Day 20

Call 5 current prospects who probably did not buy an annuity from you because of the surrender charges.

Share with them that you read a book that devoted one entire section of the book to the topic of surrender charges with annuities and the other types of penalties that bank CDs, real estate, and municipal bonds have.

Using the passion in your voice, "We have to get together so you can benefit from what I have just learned. Where would the best place be to meet this Saturday, the local library, Barnes and Noble or your place?"

Please read pages 201-221 in the book regarding surrender charges.

Kind Reminder

In the opening pages of The Next 30 Days, we gave you an important homework assignment. However, we told you that you would not need to have this assignment done until you get to Day 21. We then suggested that you hire a high school or college student and ask them to go to your file cabinet and create an Excel sheet with the following categories: 1) names of all of your clients, former clients, and current prospects, 2) the type they are like (c) for clients, (fc) for former clients and (cp) for current prospects, 3) their dates of birth, 4) their occupation and industry, like doctor/medicine, and 5) the date of the first application that you ever completed for that client or former client; just the first application.

Well it is now Day 21. As you will soon see, Days 21-30 may be the most productive days in your career and the most enjoyable too.

Day 21

Call 5 clients, former clients, and current prospects that are having a birthday today or later this week.

Share with them what things cost the day they were born* by using our inflation-fighting script, including "the best place to meet for 15 minutes close" that is on page 143 in this book.

*Use our 2 page chart in *75 Secrets* pages 348-349 that shows what things cost between 1936-1985.

Day 22

Call 5 clients, 5 former clients, and 5 current prospects who are 2 weeks away from an insurance age change.

Share with them that they will never get younger than they are today.

Proudly announce the "sale" that is on life insurance and health insurance during the days preceding their insurance age change.

Compute the lifetime difference in premiums and values between acting now versus acting after their insurance age changes.

Day 23

Call 5 current prospects who are 90 days from turning 62 who just might retire.

Share with them:

- that you just bought a $75 book that will help you help your clients

- tell them the name of the book

- that pp. 45-48 unveil Secret # 12, which is titled *It might be smarter for some to get the smaller Social Security benefit at age 62.*

Tell them that they have to see this book since it explains the 4 things they must consider and tells them on the last page which Next Steps to take.

Suggest to meet for 15 minutes at their favorite coffee shop tomorrow morning.

Day 24

Call 5 current prospects 90-100 days before their birthday.

Tell them:

- that you just bought a $75 book that will help you help your clients

- the name of the book

- that pp. 119-122 unveil Secret #30 which is titled *Review the Social Security Statement that you get every year with your professionals.*

- they have to see this book since this book breaks down their Social Security Statement in easy to understand parts

- the Social Security Administration will be mailing the statement to them 90 days before their birthday

- you want to review their Social Security statement with them by using the $75 book

Day 25

Call 5 clients and 5 former clients if this month is your anniversary together.

Remind them that years ago, on (say this month and the date on the app*), you completed your first application together, which signaled the beginning of (now say the benefits of owning your product such as tax control).

Happy Anniversary!

Ask, "Would you like to (smile in voice) celebrate our anniversary together for 15 minutes at Baskin Robbins?"

*This on your Excel sheet that your college student created for you.

Day 26

Call 5 clients who are doctors, CPAs, attorneys, and roofers.

Share with them that you are planning to call the following 10 (now say their profession).

Ask them if they know any of the them on a first name basis and begin saying their names; names that you may have gotten from the yellow pages or an association membership directory.

After learning who they know, get a little more info about each and then ask the $64,000 question, "When I give them a call, you would not mind if I mentioned that you were my client."

Please reread Secret 3 in this book about how to use our Referral folder.

Day 27

Call 5 current prospects who are 90 days within turning 66 who just might retire.

Share with them:

- that you just bought a $75 book that will help you help your clients

- tell them the name of the book

- that pp. 45-48 unveil Secret #12, which has a chart on page 47 that might help them decide on whether they should elect Social Security at age 66 or wait until age 70

Tell them that they have to see this chart plus the last page tells them the Next Steps to take.

Day 28

Call 5 prospects who are most apt to have credit card debt.

Share with them that you just bought a $75 book that will help you help your clients.

Tell them the name of book.

Read to them the short paragraph on page 135.

Share with them that this book has 74 common sense approaches, concepts, and strategies like the one on page 135.

Tell them (with passion) "You have to see this book if you want to pay less taxes, save more, and sidestep making mistakes about money."

Ask for the best place to get together for 15 minutes.

Day 29

Call 5 current prospects who are more apt to have a 401(k).

Share with them:

- that you just bought a $75 book that will help you help your clients

- tell the name of the book

- that page 312 unveils how the two of you can go online and compare the performance and fees of their 401(k) plan to 5,000 more 401(k) plans

Suggest to meet for 15 minutes at their FedEx Kinkos or at a local library so you can go online together.

Day 30

Call 5 divorced women you know who were married for 10 years but whose former husband died after the divorce.

Share with them that you just bought a $75 book that will help you help your clients.

Tell them the name of the book.

Read to them the short paragraph on page 312 that explains that they might be eligible for Social Security Survivor benefits.

Share with them that this new book has 74 common sense approaches, concepts, and strategies like the one on page 312.

Tell them (with passion) "You have to see this book if you want to pay less taxes, save more, sidestep making mistakes about money, and get everything you are entitled to."

Ask for best place to get together.

Your Next 30 Days

Now please go to page 263 Day 1 and repeat this for another 30 days.

Why should you repeat it when you have more prospects in your pipeline than ever before?

Here are reasons why you should continue:

1. We owe it to our spouse and children to be the best we can be and slowing down is not being our best. Have you ever seen a baseball player hit a triple running half speed? Said differently, give it everything you got!

2. Enjoy every sale for 5 minutes and then move on. First of all, you have to show your newest client that they made a wise decision. Secondly, you need a "new" new client asap.

What if:

   Mr. Ford wanted to sell only 500 cars?

   Mrs. Cola did not mind being in 2nd place.

   Your favorite insurance company wanted to be licensed in only 1 state.

We need go-getters who want the best for their families and their clients.

Bill Harris
President
W.V.H.,Inc

Prospecting Concepts

"Discover in minutes what took us 4 decades to learn, refine, & almost master."

Bill Harris, President, W.V.H., Inc.

Are you shooting 3 pointers or layups?

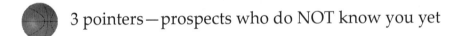 3 pointers—prospects who do NOT know you yet

 Layups—prospects who know you

Photo and Photography Credit: Shutterstock By lucadp

The Power Ranking Of Prospects
Those prospects most apt and least apt to say yes to you today

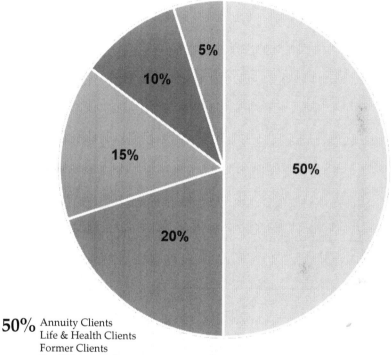

50% Annuity Clients
Life & Health Clients
Former Clients
Small Business Owners (you are their client)
Referrals (variable power)
Current Prospects (if you know their date of birth)

10% Members Of A Group
Residents In Your Community

20% Current Prospects (4 + meetings)
Guests at CAE* events
LinkedIn Connections (variable power)
Face Book Friends (variable power)
Twitter Followers (variable power)

5% Direct Mail
(with some demographic knowledge)

Cold Calls
(with some demographic knowledge)

15% Consumer Webinar Attendees
Parents Of Your Clients
Children Of Your Clients
Readers Of Your E- Book

Year	Newspaper	1st Class Stamp	Car	Home
		What Things Cost		
1936	3¢	3¢	$695	$3,825
1937	3¢	3¢	$750	$4,000
1938	3¢	3¢	$753	$3,800
1939	3¢	3¢	$867	$3,700
1940	3¢	3¢	$828	$2,938
1941	3¢	3¢	$840	$2,938
1942	3¢	3¢	*	$3,529
1943	3¢	3¢	*	$3,868
1944	3¢	3¢	*	$4,238
1945	3¢	3¢	$1,030	$4,645
1946	3¢	3¢	$1,020	$5,080
1947	5¢	3¢	$1,200	$5,577
1948	5¢	3¢	$1,660	$6,112
1949	5¢	3¢	$1,362	$6,170
1950	5¢	3¢	$1,299	$7,354
1951	5¢	3¢	$1,362	$7,113
1952	5¢	3¢	$2,065	$8,090
1953	5¢	3¢	$2,679	$8,486
1954	5¢	3¢	$2,638	$8,901
1955	5¢	3¢	$1,500	$9,337
1956	5¢	3¢	$1,367	$9,795
1957	5¢	3¢	$1,467	$10,274
1958	5¢	4¢	$1,695	$10,777
1959	5¢	4¢	$1,561	$11,305
1960	6¢	4¢	$1,627	$11,900

*N/A WWII   Sources: W.V.H., Inc.; Annapolis Capital; Morris County Library; Department of Labor; Bureau of Labor Statistics; Board of Governors of the Federal Reserve System; U.S. Census Bureau

What Things Cost				
Year	News-paper	1st Class Stamp	Car	Home
1961	6¢	4¢	$2,464	$12,340
1962	7¢	4¢	$1,595	$12,797
1963	7¢	5¢	$2,494	$13,270
1964	7¢	5¢	$1,455	$13,761
1965	10¢	5¢	$1,959	$14,270
1966	10¢	5¢	$3,399	$14,798
1967	10¢	6¢	$2,365	$15,346
1968	10¢	6¢	$2,597	$15,913
1969	10¢	6¢	$3,175	$16,501
1970	10¢	6¢	$2,652	$17,000
1971	15¢	6¢	$3,395	$18,836
1972	15¢	8¢	$2,796	$20,870
1973	15¢	8¢	$4,281	$23,124
1974	15¢	8¢	$2,408	$25,621
1975	15¢	10¢	$2,999	$28,388
1976	20¢	13¢	$3,220	$31,454
1977	20¢	13¢	$3,588	$34,849
1978	20¢	13¢	$4,299	$38,613
1979	25¢	18¢	$10,654	$42,783
1980	25¢	15¢	$8,085	$47,200
1981	25¢	15¢	$6,194	$49,654
1982	25¢	20¢	$13,491	$52,236
1983	25¢	20¢	$9,399	$54,952
1984	25¢	20¢	$13,489	$57,810
1985	25¢	22¢	$8,999	$60,815

Sources: W.V.H., Inc.; Annapolis Capital; Morris County Library; Department of Labor;
Bureau of Labor Statistics; Board of Governors of the Federal Reserve System; U.S. Census Bureau

Proven Prospecting   Formula
AMP-TB- ATST*

- Consumer Web Conferences

- Client Appreciation Events

- Seminars & Seminar Math

- Email Campaigns, LinkedIn Posts, Facebook
  & Twitter, Direct Mail, TV & Radio, Guest Speaker

Ask More People To Buy At The Same Time

Some Of The Best High Tech Platforms For Advisors To Use

Disable, Mute, Record for legal purposes & not for distribution, Duration, Guest Speaker as a co-presenter only, Best days, Best times, A/B testing subject lines, best verbs, give-aways

secondary web site, posts, search engine

Index

Index

Index

Index

More W.V.H., Inc. Products

Visit www.75 Secrets.com

75 Secrets Book: Perfect For The Insurance/Investment Professional

Description: 354-pages with the 75 best sales presentations about potentially accumulating more money for retirement. Each sales presentation (secret) is a proven approach, overlooked concept, or forgotten strategy. Each presentation is 4 pages long and includes a sales-creating point-of-sale chart, questionnaires, or outline...

Both the paperback and hard cover book also include:

- 25 great short bonus secrets,
- a Product Description section on CDs and Annuities,
- an Advantage/Disadvantage section on CDs and all types of Annuities
- and 10 extra charts for presentations.

Bonus: This book is a great companion for those who use The Next 30 Days day-to-day calendar in 7 Big Secrets to schedule appointments since you get the charts, questionnaires, etc. you will need at the point-of-sale.

Your Investment: $74.99

Audio Library Of 6 CDs For Training At Its Best (6 Hours of Recording)

Description: 6 audio CDs for your car or office with Bill Harris unveiling ALL of the CD, Annuity, and Retirement Planning secrets in the 75 Secrets book. CD #6 includes the audio recording of W.V.H., Inc.'s popular films with former Presidents of the U.S. with a behind-the-scenes commentary from Bill Harris about each film.

Listen to Bill for 1 hour everyday for 6 days and learn proven approaches, concepts, and strategies. Then re-listen to the sales presentation that you are about to give as you are driving to the appointment.

Bonus 1: The Audio CDs are very helpful since you will learn how Bill Harris would deliver the 75 sales presentations at the point-of-sale.

"How words are said, in other words, the execution and the delivery of the words are sometimes more important at the point-of-sale than the words by itself."

Bonus 2: Audio CDs are highly professional with one narrator reading the secret title, Bill unveiling the secret, and another professional narrator reading the important disclosure.

Bonus 3: Audio CDs are also slightly entertaining since they include 4 different musical scores plus short musical clips whenever Bill is outlining 3, 4, or 5 important benefits.

Your Investment: $350

Multi-Media DVD-ROM For Unforgettable Point-of-Sale Presentations

- one-on-one
- client seminars
- client appreciation events

Description :Watch Secrets come to life on video.

With Secret 75, you get 14 of W.V.H. Inc.'s best films of former Presidents of the U.S. discussing Social Security, Health Care, Economy, Income Taxes, Inflation, etc.. You also get Bill Harris at his best on video unveiling another 14 secrets.

Plus the DVD-ROM has the entire 75 Secrets book so you have lightening speed access to any page in our 75 Secrets book. (the book on the DVD-ROM is a non-printable, non-transferable PDF)   Your Investment: $350 (for a full 12 months)

Made in the USA
Lexington, KY
13 March 2018